what's cooking
one pot

edited by Tom Kitch

p

This is a Parragon Publishing book
First published in 2004

Parragon Publishing
Queen Street House
4 Queen Street
Bath BA1 1HE
United Kingdom

ISBN: 1-40542-540-7

Printed in China

NOTE

This book uses imperial, metric, and US cup measurements. Follow the same units of measurement throughout;
do not mix imperial and metric. All spoon measurements are level: teaspoons are assumed to be 5 ml
and tablespoons are assumed to be 15 ml. Unless otherwise stated, milk is assumed to be whole fat, eggs and
individual vegetables such as potatoes are medium, and pepper is freshly ground black pepper.

The times given for each recipe are an approximate guide only. The preparation times may differ according to
the techniques used by different people and the cooking times may vary as a result of the type of oven used.
Ovens should be preheated to the specified temperature. If using a fan-assisted oven, check the manufacturer's
instructions for adjusting the time and temperature. The preparation times include chilling
and marinating times, where appropriate.

Recipes using raw or very lightly cooked eggs should be avoided by infants, the elderly,
pregnant women, convalescents, and anyone suffering from an illness.

contents

introduction

With today's hectic lifestyles, it is all too easy to resort to unhealthy and expensive take-out meals and convenience foods. For a more economical and healthier alternative that is almost as easy, why not try one-pot meals for parties, Sunday lunches, or family suppers? One-pot meals include everything from traditional soups and bakes to international dishes from Persia, Mexico, and the Mediterranean, as well as delicious alcoholic desserts—you will find a dish for every occasion.

Preparing food at home can give you a great sense of satisfaction, but it can seem something of a chore, and clearing up afterward is often very tedious. If you have a busy life, one-pot meals may well be exactly what you need. Cook meals in batches and freeze, then heat in the microwave when you need them and relax for a few minutes. Running a household, holding down a job, and feeding the family can be difficult to balance, and one-pot meals are the ideal time-saving solution. They make busy lives easier, make less mess in the kitchen, and involve less chopping and peeling than many other dishes.

One-pot dishes also save on cleanup—they eliminate the need for a pan, skillet, casserole, and several serving dishes—most one-pot dishes can be served straight from the cooking pot. Try to find an attractive set of casseroles that you can serve from at the table, even when you have guests. One more advantage of not using serving dishes is that the food is kept piping hot, which saves you the fuss of warming plates in the oven.

Many one-pot meals can be frozen. Make them in large batches and freeze in family or single-serving portions, depending on your household. Casseroles and stews are great for cooking in batches: double the ingredients (making sure your pot is big enough), and when the dish is ready, simply let half cool and then freeze in a rigid container or freezer bag. Soups will freeze well and can be kept for up to 3 months. To thaw, simply remove from the freezer 12 hours before you require the dish and let stand at room temperature, or remove 24 hours before and place in the refrigerator.

EQUIPMENT

Investing in good-quality equipment is important. Poor quality pans and dishes do not cook food evenly, and are difficult to clean. The most important cookware for one-pot cooking are casserole dishes, skillets, and pans. When making casseroles and pot roasts, you need a dish large enough to give the ingredients room to cook, but not so much room that they dry out.

If you are planning to cook lots of casseroles and stews, a flameproof casserole will be your best buy. A solid, heavy-bottomed casserole can be expensive, but is worth the cost, as meals will be evenly cooked and flavorsome. A cast-iron casserole is best, but remember that they are very heavy when full.

Woks, skillets, and karahis (the Indian version of a wok) are also used for one-pot dishes, especially for stir-frying. Roasting pans are also important for

cooking one-pot roasts, with the vegetables sizzling in the juices from the meat. You may prefer a nonstick lining, but whatever type you choose, make sure that it is solid and large, and that the sides are of an adequate height, or you may find that cooking juices drip dangerously over the rim.

You should think about the dishes you plan to cook and, therefore, the type of pan you will find most useful. If you cook on an electric stove with a flat surface, select a wok with a flat bottom, for example. A thick, solid bottom is important to allow even distribution of heat. If the manufacturer's instructions tell you to season a pan before use, do so, because this improves the quality of cooking and the pan's lifespan.

You will probably already have most of the other necessary utensils, but there may be some, such as a zester, that you might need to buy. Using a zester is far easier than trying to grate lemon or orange rind and then scrape it from the inside of the grater. They are inexpensive and readily available. Cutting boards are an essential item and will last a long time. Whether you prefer wood or plastic, select a good, solid board that will not slip easily. Remember to use a separate board for raw meat. It is now thought that you should avoid cleaning utensils with antibacterial products, as various strains of bacteria can become completely resistant. Hot soapy water is adequate for all pans and utensils; soak them first if there is burned food on the bottom.

Measuring cups and spoons with clear, easy-to-read numbers are essential. Although you can estimate amounts with many casseroles and stews, some dishes require exact measurements. Make sure you have a full set of cups and imperial or metric measuring equipment and remember that the two systems are not interchangeable.

Other tools you will need include a perforated spoon for draining and serving—very valuable in one-pot cooking when you need to remove the meat ahead of the sauce. Find a good set of plastic utensils for nonstick surfaces or stainless steel for other dishes—these will last for years. A pestle and mortar is a necessity if you like to use fresh spices, which add a better flavor and color than ready-ground ones.

Good-quality, sharp knives make life a lot easier, saving time and increasing safety in the kitchen. You should also buy a knife sharpener—using blunt knives is dangerous. A carving knife is ideal for carving pot roasts and other pieces of meat. A large chopping knife with a heavy blade is useful for a multitude of purposes, but you may find a range of different knives suits you. A paring knife is smaller and lighter and is perfect for trimming, peeling, and chopping small vegetables.

Nowadays, there are ways to speed up preparation times. For a real timesaver, invest in a food processor—a good-quality one will last for a long time. Alternatively, most supermarkets now stock a range of washed, peeled, and chopped vegetables, such as carrots, baby corn, asparagus, and salads, as well as canned goods. Canned foods are not so fresh as the ready-prepared varieties and often have little flavor and color, but some types, such as tomatoes, beans, peas, and lentils, are invaluable.

THE PANTRY

Although fresh vegetables have a unique flavor and texture, there are alternatives that can make a delicious last-minute supper. Keep your pantry well stocked to prevent a last-minute rush to the store. Ingredients in jars or cans will save on preparation time, too—most things can be bought chopped, peeled, or flavored at little or no extra cost. Improvise by using chickpeas when the recipe calls for kidney beans, and for new dishes experiment by using the ingredients buried at the back of the pantry. Most of us have basics, such as pasta, rice, and canned tomatoes, but next time you go shopping, spend some time in the canned food aisle and select a few more unusual ingredients to try.

soups

There is something especially appetizing about homemade soup. Most of the soups in this chapter make a filling first course or, served with some fresh rolls or crusty bread, a light lunch or evening snack.

It is worth making your own stock—and that's only one pot, too—because that way, you can be sure of the quality and flavor. Chicken stock is a good all-round basic, if you don't want to bother making several different types, and it can even be used for fish soups. If you do have to use bouillon cubes, look for ones with a low salt content and be careful when you season the soup.

In this chapter, there are spicy soups from Asia, hearty country soups from France, and fabulous fish soups from both home and the Mediterranean. There are familiar family favorites, such as Bacon & Lentil Soup (see page 16), and some more unusual ideas, such as Cheese & Vegetable Chowder (see page 32). All are easy to make and some are surprisingly quick, so you are sure to find one to please you and your family.

cock-a-leekie

serves 6

5 minutes

2 hours 40 minutes

1 chicken, weighing about 3 lb/1.3 kg
2 quarts beef stock
2 lb/900 g leeks
1 bouquet garni
salt and pepper

2 cups prunes, pitted and
soaked overnight in enough
cold water to cover

*Two for the price of one—serve the
soup separately as a first course
and the meat and vegetables as an
entrée. Alternatively, for a really
chunky dish, ladle the whole thing
into large soup plates.*

cook's tip

*A bouquet garni usually consists of
3 fresh parsley sprigs, 2 fresh
thyme sprigs, and a bay leaf, tied
together in a bundle.*

Put the chicken, breast-side down, into a large, heavy-bottomed pan or flameproof casserole. Pour in the stock and bring to a boil, skimming off any foam that rises to the surface.

Tie half the leeks together in a bundle with kitchen string and thinly slice the remainder. Add the bundle of leeks to the pan with the bouquet garni and a pinch of salt, reduce the heat, partially cover, and simmer for 2 hours, or until the chicken is tender.

Remove and discard the bundle of leeks and bouquet garni. Drain the prunes, add them to the pan, and simmer for 20 minutes. Season to taste with salt and pepper and add the sliced leeks. Simmer for an additional 10 minutes. Slice the chicken, or cut into bite-size pieces, and serve the soup immediately.

thai COCONUT soup

serves 4

10 minutes

55 minutes

1 quart chicken stock

7 oz/200 g skinless, boneless chicken

1 fresh chile, split lengthwise and seeded

3-inch/7.5-cm piece lemon grass, split lengthwise

3–4 lime leaves

1-inch/2.5-cm piece fresh gingerroot, peeled and sliced

½ cup coconut milk

6–8 scallions, sliced diagonally

¼ tsp chili paste, to taste

salt

fresh cilantro leaves, to garnish

This soup makes a change from traditional chicken soup. It is spicy, and garnished with a generous quantity of fresh cilantro.

cook's tip

Once the stock is flavored and the chicken cooked, this soup is very quick to finish. If you wish, poach the chicken and strain the stock ahead of time. Store in the refrigerator separately.

Put the stock into a pan with the chicken, chile, lemon grass, lime leaves, and gingerroot. Bring almost to a boil, then reduce the heat, cover, and simmer for 20–25 minutes, or until the chicken is cooked through.

Remove the chicken from the pan and strain the stock. When the chicken is cool, thinly slice or shred into bite-size pieces.

Return the stock to the pan and heat to simmering. Stir in the coconut milk and scallions. Add the chicken and continue simmering for 10 minutes, or until the soup is heated through and the flavors have mingled.

Stir in the chili paste. Season to taste with salt and, if wished, add a little more chili paste.

Ladle into warmed bowls and float cilantro leaves on top to serve.

chicken, corn & bean soup

serves 6

10 minutes

45 minutes

1½ tbsp butter
1 large onion, finely chopped
1 garlic clove, finely chopped
3 tbsp all-purpose flour
2½ cups water
4 cups chicken stock
1 carrot, quartered and thinly sliced

6 oz/175 g green beans,
 cut into short pieces
14 oz/400 g canned lima beans,
 drained and rinsed
3 cups cooked or frozen corn
8 oz/225 g cooked chicken meat
salt and pepper

This soup is especially tasty using fresh corn kernels cut from 3 or 4 corn cobs. However, frozen corn is a quick and easy alternative.

variation

Replace the lima beans with 10½ oz/300 g cooked fresh fava beans, peeled if wished. You could also substitute sliced string beans for the green beans.

Melt the butter in a large pan over medium-low heat. Add the chopped onion and garlic and cook, stirring frequently, for 3–4 minutes, or until just softened.

Stir in the flour and continue cooking for 2 minutes, stirring occasionally.

Gradually pour in the water, stirring constantly and scraping the bottom of the pan to mix in the flour. Bring to a boil, stirring frequently, and cook for 2 minutes. Add the stock and stir until smooth.

Add the carrot, green beans, lima beans, corn, and chicken meat. Season to taste with salt and pepper. Bring back to a boil, then reduce the heat to medium-low, cover, and simmer for 35 minutes, or until the vegetables are tender.

Taste the soup and adjust the seasoning, adding salt, if needed, and plenty of pepper.

Ladle the soup into warmed, deep bowls and serve.

frankfurter &
split pea broth

serves 6

**15 minutes,
plus 2 hours soaking**

2 hours 15 minutes

8 oz/225 g salt belly of pork,
    cut into cubes

2¼ quarts water

2¾ cups split peas, soaked
    in enough cold water to cover
    for 2 hours

4 onions, chopped

2 leeks, chopped

4 carrots, chopped

4 celery stalks, chopped

1 cooking apple, peeled,
    cored, and chopped

1 tbsp raw brown sugar

1 bouquet garni

6 frankfurters, cut into
    1-inch/2.5-cm lengths

2 tbsp butter

salt and pepper

celery leaves, to garnish

*Economical, nourishing, filling, and
packed with flavor—what more
could you ask for on a chilly
winter's evening?*

Put the pork cubes into a large, heavy-bottomed pan and add enough cold water to cover. Bring to a boil over low heat, then drain well. Return the pork to the pan and add the measured water.

Drain and rinse the split peas, then add them to the pan with the onions, leeks, carrots, celery, apple, sugar, and bouquet garni. Bring to a boil, skimming off any foam that rises to the surface. Reduce the heat, cover, and simmer, stirring occasionally, for 2 hours.

Remove and discard the bouquet garni and stir in the frankfurters and butter. Season to taste with salt and pepper and heat through. Ladle into warmed bowls, garnish with celery leaves, and serve immediately.

cook's tip

*You can use yellow or green
split peas for this soup. The cooking
time may vary depending on their
freshness—the fresher they are,
the quicker they will cook.*

variation

*Substitute other favorite vegetables,
such as parsnips and bell peppers,
for the carrots and celery, if
you prefer.*

bacon & lentil soup

serves 4

15 minutes

1 hour 10 minutes

1 lb/450 g thick, rindless smoked
   bacon slices, diced
1 onion, chopped
2 carrots, sliced
2 celery stalks, chopped
1 turnip, chopped

1 large potato, chopped
scant ½ cup Puy lentils
1 bouquet garni
4 cups water or
   chicken stock
salt and pepper

*Bacon and lentils have a real
affinity—their flavors and
textures complement one
another. This popular family
supper also includes a selection
of tasty winter vegetables.*

Heat a large, heavy-bottomed pan or flameproof casserole. Add the bacon
and cook over medium heat, stirring, for 4–5 minutes, or until the fat runs.
Add the chopped onion, carrots, celery, turnip, and potato and cook,
stirring frequently, for 5 minutes.

Add the lentils and bouquet garni and pour in the water or stock. Bring
the soup to a boil, then reduce the heat and simmer for 1 hour, or until
the lentils are tender.

Remove and discard the bouquet garni and season the soup to taste with
pepper and salt, if necessary. Ladle into warmed soup bowls and serve.

cook's tip

*Do not add any salt until the lentils
have finished cooking, otherwise
they will toughen, which will impair
the texture of the soup.*

variation

*You can use different root
vegetables, such as rutabaga and
parsnips, instead of the carrots and
turnips, if you prefer.*

pork chili soup

serves 3

10 minutes

55 minutes

2 tsp olive oil
1 lb 2 oz/500 g lean ground pork
salt and pepper
1 onion, finely chopped
1 celery stalk, finely chopped
1 bell pepper, seeded and
  finely chopped
2–3 garlic cloves, finely chopped
14 oz/400 g canned chopped
  tomatoes in juice

3 tbsp tomato paste
2 cups chicken or
  meat stock
1/4 tsp ground coriander
1/4 tsp ground cumin
1/4 tsp dried oregano
1 tsp mild chili powder
chopped fresh cilantro
  or parsley, to garnish
sour cream, to serve

This meaty chili tastes lighter than one made with beef. Good for informal entertaining, the recipe is easily doubled.

cook's tip

For a festive presentation, serve additional accompaniments, such as grated cheese, chopped scallions, and guacamole.

Heat the oil in a large pan over medium-high heat. Add the pork, season to taste with salt and pepper, and cook, stirring frequently, until no longer pink. Reduce the heat to medium and add the onion, celery, bell pepper, and garlic. Cover and cook, stirring occasionally, for an additional 5 minutes until the onion is softened.

Add the tomatoes, tomato paste, and the stock. Stir in the coriander, cumin, oregano, and chili powder. Season to taste with salt and pepper.

Bring just to a boil, then reduce the heat to low, cover, and simmer for 30–40 minutes, or until all the vegetables are very tender. Taste and adjust the seasoning, adding more chili powder if you like it hotter.

Ladle the chili into warmed bowls and sprinkle with chopped cilantro or parsley. You can either hand round the sour cream separately or top each serving with a spoonful.

leek, potato & bacon soup

serves 4

15 minutes

25 minutes

2 tbsp butter
6 oz/175 g potatoes, diced
4 leeks, shredded
2 garlic cloves, crushed
3½ oz/100 g smoked bacon, diced
3½ cups vegetable stock

1 cup heavy cream
2 tbsp chopped fresh parsley
salt and pepper

to garnish
vegetable oil
1 leek, shredded

Leek and potato soup is a classic recipe. Here the soup is enhanced with smoked bacon pieces and enriched with heavy cream for a little luxury.

Melt the butter in a large pan and add the diced potatoes, shredded leeks, garlic, and diced bacon. Sauté gently for 5 minutes, stirring constantly.

Add the stock and bring to a boil. Reduce the heat, cover, and simmer for 20 minutes until the potatoes are cooked. Stir in the heavy cream.

Meanwhile, make the garnish. Half-fill a pan with oil and heat to 350–375°F/180–190°C, or until a cube of bread browns in 30 seconds. Add the shredded leek and deep-fry for 1 minute until browned and crisp, taking care as the leek contains water and may cause the oil to spatter. Drain the leek thoroughly on paper towels and reserve.

variation

For a lighter soup, omit the cream and stir plain yogurt into the soup at the end of the cooking time.

Reserve a few pieces of potato, leek, and bacon and set aside. Put the rest of the soup in a food processor or blender in batches and process each batch for 30 seconds. Return the puréed soup to a clean pan and heat through.

Stir in the reserved vegetables and bacon and chopped parsley. Season to taste with salt and pepper. Pour into warmed bowls and garnish with the deep-fried leeks.

spicy lamb soup

with zucchini

serves 4–5

10 minutes

about 1 hour 50 minutes

1–2 tbsp olive oil

1 lb/450 g lean boneless lamb, such as shoulder or neck fillet, trimmed of fat and cut into 1/2-inch/1-cm cubes

1 onion, finely chopped

2–3 garlic cloves, crushed

1 quart water

14 oz/400 g canned chopped tomatoes in juice

1 bay leaf

1/2 tsp dried thyme

1/2 tsp dried oregano

pinch of ground cinnamon

1/4 tsp ground cumin

1/4 tsp ground turmeric

1 tsp harissa (see Cook's Tip)

14 oz/400 g canned chickpeas, drained and rinsed

1 carrot, diced

1 potato, diced

1 zucchini, quartered lengthwise and sliced

scant 1 cup fresh or thawed frozen peas

salt and pepper

chopped fresh mint or cilantro, to garnish

Packed with tomatoes, chickpeas, and vegetables, this thick and hearty main-course soup is bursting with exotic flavors and aromas.

Heat the oil in a large pan or flameproof casserole over medium-high heat. Add the lamb, in batches if necessary, and cook, stirring occasionally, until evenly browned on all sides, adding a little more oil if needed. Remove the meat with a perforated spoon.

Reduce the heat and add the onion and garlic to the pan. Cook, stirring frequently, for 1–2 minutes.

Add the water and return all the meat to the pan. Bring just to a boil and skim off any foam that rises to the surface. Reduce the heat and stir in the tomatoes, bay leaf, thyme, oregano, cinnamon, cumin, turmeric, and harissa. Simmer for 1 hour, or until the meat is very tender. Discard the bay leaf.

cook's tip

Harissa is a spicy North African sauce, made with olive oil, chiles, garlic, coriander, and other spices. It is available in supermarkets.

Stir in the chickpeas, carrot, and potato and simmer for 15 minutes. Add the zucchini and peas and simmer for an additional 15–20 minutes, or until all the vegetables are tender.

Season to taste with salt and pepper and add more harissa if desired. Ladle the soup into warmed bowls, garnish with chopped fresh mint or cilantro, and serve immediately.

scotch broth

serves 4–6

about 10 minutes

1 hour 25 minutes

generous ¼ cup pearl barley

10½ oz/300 g lean boneless lamb, such as shoulder or neck fillet, trimmed of fat and cut into ½-inch/1-cm cubes

3 cups water

2 garlic cloves, finely chopped or crushed

4 cups chicken or meat stock

1 onion, finely chopped

1 bay leaf

1 large leek, quartered lengthwise and sliced

2 large carrots, finely diced

1 parsnip, finely diced

4½ oz/125 g rutabaga, diced

salt and pepper

2 tbsp chopped fresh parsley

This traditional winter soup is full of goodness, with lots of tasty golden vegetables along with tender barley and lamb.

cook's tip

By making this soup beforehand, you can cut the calories by removing any hardened fat before reheating.

Rinse the barley under cold running water. Put in a pan and add water to cover generously. Bring to a boil over medium heat and boil for 3 minutes, skimming off any foam that rises to the surface. Remove the pan from the heat, cover, and set aside.

Put the lamb in a separate large pan with the water and bring to a boil. Skim off any foam that rises to the surface.

Stir in the garlic, stock, onion, and bay leaf. Reduce the heat, partially cover, and simmer for 15 minutes.

Drain the barley and add to the soup. Add the leek, carrots, parsnip, and rutabaga. Simmer, stirring occasionally, for 1 hour, or until the lamb and vegetables are tender.

Season to taste with salt and pepper, stir in the parsley, and serve.

vegetable beef soup

serves 6–8

10 minutes

2 hours 10 minutes

1 lb/450 g stewing steak
1 lb 12 oz/800 g canned chopped tomatoes in juice
2 onions, finely chopped
2–3 garlic cloves, finely chopped
3 carrots, diced
2 celery stalks, sliced
5½ oz/150 g green cabbage, thinly sliced
1 bay leaf

5–6 allspice berries
¼ tsp dried thyme
¼ tsp dried marjoram
4 cups water
4 cups beef stock
salt and pepper
7 oz/200 g green beans, cut into short pieces
1⅓ cups peas
1⅓ cups corn

This soup is hearty and warming. It's a wonderful way to use fresh garden produce, but frozen vegetables are equally colorful and nutritious. No need to thaw them first.

cook's tip

For quick beef stock, dilute 1 bouillon cube in 4 cups water, or use a can of beef consommé made up to that quantity with water. Alternatively, you can use all water and add 1 teaspoon salt.

Trim all visible fat from the steak and cut into ½-inch/1-cm cubes. Put into a large pan with the tomatoes, onions, garlic, carrots, celery, cabbage, bay leaf, allspice, thyme, marjoram, and water.

Bring to a boil over medium-high heat, skimming off any foam that rises to the surface. Stir in the stock, reduce the heat, and regulate it so that the soup boils very gently. Season to taste with salt and pepper. Cook, partially covered, for 1 hour, stirring occasionally.

Add the green beans, peas, and corn. Continue cooking for an additional hour, or until the meat and vegetables are very tender.

Taste and adjust the seasoning, if necessary. Ladle into warmed bowls and serve immediately.

french onion soup

serves 6

5–10 minutes

1 hour 40 minutes

1 tbsp butter

2 tbsp olive oil

2 lb 4 oz/1 kg large yellow onions, halved and sliced into half-circles

3 large garlic cloves, finely chopped

salt and pepper

2 tbsp all-purpose flour

scant 1 cup dry white wine

1¾ quarts beef stock

3 tbsp brandy

6 slices French bread

7 oz/200 g Gruyère cheese, grated

A rich, flavorsome homemade stock is the key to this satisfying soup. While beef stock is traditional, a rich, intense chicken stock would be delicious as well.

cook's tip

Don't try to hurry this soup. The rich flavor comes from cooking the onions slowly so that their natural sugar caramelizes, then adding the well-flavored stock.

Melt the butter with the oil in a large, heavy-bottomed pan over medium heat. Add the onions and cook, covered, for 10–12 minutes, or until they soften, stirring occasionally. Add the garlic and salt and pepper to taste.

Reduce the heat a little and continue cooking, uncovered, for 30–35 minutes, or until the onions turn a deep, golden brown, stirring from time to time until they start to color, then stirring more frequently and scraping the bottom of the pan as they begin to stick (see Cook's Tip).

Sprinkle over the flour and stir to blend. Stir in the white wine and bubble for 1 minute. Pour in the stock and bring to a boil, scraping the bottom of the pan and stirring to combine well. Reduce the heat to low, add the brandy, and simmer gently, stirring occasionally, for 45 minutes.

Toast the bread under a preheated hot broiler on one side. Turn over and top with the cheese, dividing it evenly. Broil until the cheese melts.

Place a piece of cheese toast in each of the 6 warmed bowls, then ladle the hot soup over. Serve at once.

green vegetable soup
with basil pesto

serves 6

5–10 minutes

45 minutes

1 tbsp olive oil
1 onion, finely chopped
1 large leek, split and thinly sliced
1 celery stalk, thinly sliced
1 carrot, quartered and thinly sliced
1 garlic clove, finely chopped
1 1/4 quarts water
1 potato, diced
1 parsnip, finely diced
1 small kohlrabi or turnip, diced
5 1/2 oz/150 g French beans, cut into short pieces
1 1/3 cups fresh or frozen peas

2 small zucchini, quartered lengthwise and sliced
14 oz/400 g canned flageolet beans, drained and rinsed
salt and pepper
3 1/2 oz/100 g spinach leaves, cut into thin ribbons

pesto

1 large garlic clove, very finely chopped
1/2 oz/15 g basil leaves
3 oz/85 g Parmesan cheese, grated
4 tbsp extra virgin olive oil

This soup takes advantage of summer vegetables bursting with flavor. If you find fresh flageolets or other fresh beans, be sure to include them.

Heat the oil in a large pan. Add the onion and leek and cook over low heat, stirring occasionally, for 5 minutes. Add the celery, carrot, and garlic, cover, and cook for an additional 5 minutes.

Add the water, potato, parsnip, kohlrabi or turnip, and green beans. Bring to a boil, then reduce the heat, cover, and simmer for 5 minutes.

Add the peas, zucchini, and flageolet beans and season to taste with salt and pepper. Cover and simmer for 25 minutes, or until all the vegetables are tender.

Meanwhile, make the pesto. Put all the ingredients into a food processor and process until smooth, scraping down the sides as necessary. Alternatively, pound together using a pestle and mortar.

Add the spinach to the soup and simmer for 5 minutes. Stir a spoonful of the pesto into the soup. Ladle into warmed bowls and hand round the remaining pesto separately.

cheese & vegetable
chowder

serves 4

15 minutes

about 55 minutes

2 tbsp butter

1 large onion, finely chopped

1 large leek, split lengthwise and thinly sliced

1–2 garlic cloves, crushed

scant $1/2$ cup all-purpose flour

1 quart vegetable stock

3 carrots, finely diced

2 celery stalks, finely diced

1 turnip, finely diced

1 large potato, finely diced

3–4 fresh thyme sprigs or $1/8$ tsp dried thyme

1 bay leaf

$1^1/2$ cups light cream

$10^1/2$ oz/300 g sharp Cheddar cheese, grated

salt and pepper

chopped fresh parsley, to garnish

This hearty soup is wonderful made in the middle of winter with fresh seasonal vegetables. Use a really well-flavored sharp Cheddar cheese.

Melt the butter in a large, heavy-bottomed pan over low–medium heat. Add the onion, leek, and garlic. Cover and cook for 5 minutes, stirring frequently, or until the vegetables are starting to soften.

Stir the flour into the vegetables and continue cooking for 2 minutes. Add a little of the stock and stir well, scraping the bottom of the pan to mix in the flour. Bring to a boil, stirring frequently, and slowly stir in the remaining stock.

Add the carrots, celery, turnip, potato, thyme, and bay leaf. Reduce the heat, cover, and cook the soup gently, stirring occasionally, for 35 minutes, or until the vegetables are tender. Remove the bay leaf and the thyme sprigs, if using.

Stir in the cream and simmer over very low heat for 5 minutes.

Add the cheese a handful at a time, stirring constantly for 1 minute after each addition to make sure it is completely melted. Do not boil. Taste the soup and adjust the seasoning, adding salt if needed, and pepper to taste.

Ladle the soup immediately into warmed bowls, sprinkle with chopped fresh parsley, and serve.

spicy potato & chickpea soup

serves 4

50 minutes

about 50 minutes

1 tbsp olive oil

1 large onion, finely chopped

2–3 garlic cloves, finely chopped or crushed

1 carrot, quartered and thinly sliced

12 oz/350 g potatoes, diced

1/4 tsp ground turmeric

1/4 tsp garam masala

1/4 tsp mild curry powder

14 oz/400 g canned chopped tomatoes in juice

3 1/2 cups water

1/4 tsp chili paste, or to taste

salt and pepper

14 oz/400 g canned chickpeas, drained and rinsed

3/4 cup fresh or frozen peas

chopped fresh cilantro, to garnish

This spicy and substantial soup uses ingredients you are likely to have on hand and makes a delicious meal-in-a-bowl.

Heat the oil in a large pan over medium heat. Add the onion and garlic and cook for 3–4 minutes, stirring occasionally, or until the onion is beginning to soften.

Add the carrot, potatoes, turmeric, garam masala, and curry powder and continue cooking for 1–2 minutes.

Add the tomatoes, water, and chili paste with a pinch of salt. Reduce the heat, cover, and simmer for 30 minutes, stirring occasionally.

Add the chickpeas and peas to the pan, then simmer for an additional 15 minutes, or until all the vegetables are tender.

Taste the soup and adjust the seasoning, if necessary, adding a little more chili if desired. Ladle into warmed soup bowls and sprinkle with cilantro.

salmon & leek soup

serves 4

5 minutes

about 30 minutes

1 tbsp olive oil

1 large onion, finely chopped

3 large leeks, including green parts, thinly sliced

1 potato, finely diced

2 cups fish stock

3 cups water

1 bay leaf

salt and pepper

10½ oz/300 g skinless salmon fillet, cut into ½-inch/1-cm cubes

5 tbsp heavy cream

fresh lemon juice (optional)

chopped fresh chervil or parsley, to garnish

Salmon is a favorite with almost everyone. This delicately flavored and appealing soup is perfect for entertaining.

Heat the oil in a heavy-based pan over medium heat. Add the onion and leeks and cook for 3 minutes, or until they begin to soften.

Add the potato, stock, water, and bay leaf with a large pinch of salt. Bring to a boil, then reduce the heat, cover, and cook gently for 25 minutes, or until the vegetables are tender. Remove the bay leaf.

Let the soup cool slightly, then transfer about half of it to a blender or food processor and purée until smooth. (If using a food processor, strain off the cooking liquid and reserve. Purée half the soup solids with enough cooking liquid to moisten them, then combine with the remaining liquid.)

Return the puréed soup to the pan and stir to blend. Reheat gently over medium-low heat.

Season the salmon to taste with salt and pepper and add to the soup. Continue cooking for 5 minutes, stirring occasionally, or until the fish is tender and starts to break up. Stir in the cream and taste and adjust the seasoning, adding a little lemon juice, if wished. Ladle into warmed bowls, sprinkle with chervil or parsley, and serve.

smoked haddock & potato soup

serves 4

5–10 minutes

40 minutes

1 tbsp oil
2 oz/55 g smoked streaky bacon,
   cut into short, thin sticks
1 large onion, finely chopped
2 tbsp all-purpose flour
4 cups milk

1 lb 9 oz/700 g potatoes, cubed
salt and pepper
6 oz/175 g skinless smoked haddock
finely chopped fresh parsley,
   to garnish

This chunky, aromatic soup is perfect for a cold-weather lunch or supper served with crusty bread and a salad.

Heat the oil in a large pan over medium heat. Add the pieces of bacon and cook them for 2 minutes. Stir in the onion and continue cooking, stirring frequently, for 5–7 minutes, or until the onion is soft and the bacon is a golden color. Tip the pan and spoon off as much fat as possible.

Stir in the flour and continue cooking for 2 minutes. Add half of the milk and stir well, scraping the bottom of the pan to mix in the flour.

Add the potatoes and remaining milk and season to taste with pepper. Bring just to a boil, stirring frequently, then reduce the heat and simmer, partially covered, for 10 minutes.

Add the fish and continue cooking, stirring occasionally, for 15 minutes, or until the potatoes are tender and the fish breaks up easily.

Taste the soup and adjust the seasoning if necessary (salt may not be needed). Ladle into a warmed tureen or soup bowls and sprinkle with chopped parsley.

cook's tip

Cutting the potatoes into small cubes not only looks attractive— it also allows them to cook more quickly and evenly.

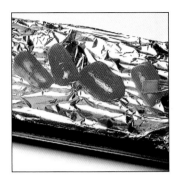  

bouillabaisse

serves 6–8

about 10 minutes

35 minutes

5 tbsp olive oil

2 large onions, finely chopped

1 leek, finely chopped

4 garlic cloves, crushed

½ small fennel bulb, finely chopped

5 ripe tomatoes, peeled and chopped

1 fresh thyme sprig

2 orange rind strips

salt and pepper

1½ quarts hot fish stock

4 lb 8oz/2 kg mixed fish, such as tilapia, red snapper, sea bass, pompano, cod, skate, soft shell crabs, raw shrimp, coarsely

chopped into equal-size pieces (shellfish left whole)

12–18 thick slices French bread

red bell pepper and saffron sauce

1 red bell pepper, seeded and quartered

⅔ cup light olive oil

1 egg yolk

large pinch of saffron

pinch of dried chili flakes

lemon juice, to taste

salt and pepper

As with many traditional French fish stews and soups, the fish and soup are served separately with a strongly flavored sauce passed around to accompany them.

To begin, make the sauce. Brush the red bell pepper quarters with a little of the light olive oil. Put under a preheated hot broiler and cook for 5–6 minutes on each side until charred and tender. Remove from the heat and transfer to a plastic bag until cool enough to handle. Peel the skins away.

Put the pepper pieces into a food processor with the egg yolk, saffron, chili flakes, lemon juice, and salt and pepper to taste and process until smooth. Begin adding the remaining light olive oil, drop by drop, until the mixture begins to thicken. Continue adding the oil in a steady stream until it is all incorporated and the mixture is thick.

In a large pan, heat the olive oil, add the onions, leek, garlic, and fennel and cook for 10–15 minutes, or until softened and starting to color. Add the tomatoes, thyme, orange rind, and salt and pepper to taste and fry for an additional 5 minutes until the tomatoes have collapsed.

Add the stock and bring to a boil. Reduce the heat and simmer gently for 10 minutes until all the vegetables are tender. Add the fish and return to a boil, then simmer gently for 10 minutes until all the fish is tender.

Toast the bread on both sides. Divide the fish between serving plates. Add some of the soup to moisten and serve with the bread. Hand round the sauce to accompany. Serve the remaining soup separately.

thai-style seafood soup

serves 4

5 minutes

about 25 minutes

1 quart fish stock

1 lemon grass stalk, split lengthwise

pared rind of ½ lime or 1 lime leaf

1-inch/2.5-cm piece fresh gingerroot, sliced

¼ tsp chili paste

4–6 scallions

7 oz/200 g medium or large raw shrimp, shelled and deveined

salt

9 oz/250 g raw prepared scallops (about 16–20)

2 tbsp chopped fresh cilantro

finely chopped red bell pepper or fresh red chile rings, to garnish

As taste and tolerance for chiles varies, using chili paste instead of fresh chiles offers more control of its strength.

variation

Substitute very small baby leeks, slivered or thinly sliced diagonally, for the scallions. Include the green parts.

Put the stock into a pan with the lemon grass, lime rind or lime leaf, gingerroot, and chili paste. Bring just to a boil, then reduce the heat, cover, and simmer for 10–15 minutes.

Cut the scallions in half lengthwise, then slice crosswise very thinly. Cut the shrimp almost in half lengthwise, keeping the tails intact.

Strain the stock, return to the pan, and bring to a simmer, with bubbles rising at the edges and the surface trembling. Add the scallions and cook for 2–3 minutes. Taste and season with salt, if needed, and stir in a little more chili paste if wished.

Add the scallops and shrimp and poach for 1 minute, or until they turn opaque and the shrimp curl.

Add the cilantro, ladle the soup into warmed bowls, and garnish with chopped red bell pepper or chile rings.

meat & poultry

This chapter is packed with main-course recipes that are sure to tempt your appetite and set your taste buds tingling. Whether your preference is for hot and spicy, rich and luxurious, or delicate and subtle flavors, you will be spoiled for choice.

Most of these dishes don't take long to prepare. Some are also cooked quite quickly, while others can be left to their own devices, bubbling gently in the kitchen while you have a well-earned rest. Remember that most stews and casseroles taste even more flavorsome if they are allowed to cool after cooking and are reheated the next day—and you still have only one pot to clean.

This chapter features a wonderful collection of economical, filling, and tasty dishes that are ideal for midweek family suppers and Sunday lunches. Equally, you need look no further for some superb suggestions for entertaining in style—whether the sophisticated spiciness of Lamb Biryani (see page 76) or the timeless elegance of Daube of Beef (see page 54).

beef & potato goulash

serves 4

10–15 minutes

about 2 hours

2 tbsp vegetable oil

1 large onion, sliced

2 garlic cloves, crushed

1 lb 10 oz/750 g lean stewing steak

2 tbsp paprika

14 oz/400 g canned chopped tomatoes

2 tbsp tomato paste

1 large red bell pepper, seeded and chopped

6 oz/175 g mushrooms, sliced

2½ cups beef stock

1 lb 2 oz/500 g potatoes, cut into large chunks

1 tbsp cornstarch

salt and pepper

to garnish

4 tbsp lowfat plain yogurt

paprika

chopped fresh parsley

In this recipe, the potatoes are actually cooked in the goulash. For a change, you may prefer to substitute small, scrubbed new potatoes.

Heat the oil in a large pan. Add the onion and garlic and cook over medium heat, stirring occasionally, for 3–4 minutes until softened.

Cut the steak into chunks, add to the pan, and cook over high heat for 3 minutes, or until browned all over.

Reduce the heat to medium and stir in the paprika. Add the tomatoes, tomato paste, red bell pepper, and mushrooms. Cook the mixture, stirring constantly, for 2 minutes.

Pour in the stock. Bring to a boil, stirring occasionally, then reduce the heat to low. Cover and simmer gently for 1½ hours, or until the meat is cooked through and tender.

Add the potatoes, cover, and cook for an additional 20–30 minutes, or until the potatoes are tender.

Blend the cornstarch with a little water and add to the pan, stirring until thickened and blended. Cook for 1 minute, then season to taste with salt and pepper. Top with the yogurt, sprinkle over paprika and chopped fresh parsley, and serve immediately.

beef in beer with herb dumplings

serves 6

5–10 minutes

2 hours 30 minutes

stew

2 tbsp corn oil

2 large onions, thinly sliced

8 carrots, sliced

4 tbsp all-purpose flour

salt and pepper

2 lb 12 oz/1.25 kg stewing steak, cut into cubes

generous 1 3/4 cups stout

2 tsp raw brown sugar

2 bay leaves

1 tbsp chopped fresh thyme

dumplings

generous 3/4 cup self-rising flour

salt

1/2 cup shredded suet

2 tbsp chopped fresh parsley, plus extra to garnish

about 4 tbsp water

Serve this traditional stew with its topping of satisfying dumplings to counteract even the coldest winter weather.

variation

Substitute other root vegetables, such as chopped parsnips or turnips for the sliced carrots, if you prefer.

Preheat the oven to 325°F/160°C. Heat the oil in a flameproof casserole. Add the onions and carrots and cook over low heat, stirring occasionally, for 5 minutes, or until the onions are softened. Meanwhile, put the flour into a plastic bag and season to taste with salt and pepper. Add the stewing steak to the bag, tie the top, and shake well to coat. Do this in batches, if necessary.

Remove the vegetables from the casserole with a perforated spoon and reserve. Add the steak to the casserole, in batches, and cook, stirring frequently, until browned all over. Return all the meat and the onions and carrots to the casserole and sprinkle in any remaining seasoned flour. Pour in the stout and add the sugar, bay leaves, and thyme. Bring to a boil, cover, and cook in the preheated oven for 1 3/4 hours.

To make the dumplings, sift the flour with a pinch of salt into a bowl. Stir in the suet and parsley and add enough of the water to make a soft dough. Shape into small balls between the palms of your hands. Add to the casserole and return to the oven for 30 minutes. Remove and discard the bay leaves and serve, sprinkled with chopped parsley.

rich beef stew

serves 4

10 minutes,
plus 30 minutes soaking

1 hour 45 minutes

1 tbsp vegetable oil
1 tbsp butter
8 oz/225 g pearl onions, peeled
  and halved
1 lb 5 oz/600 g stewing steak, diced
  into 1¹/₂-inch/4-cm cubes
1¹/₄ cups beef stock
²/₃ cup red wine

4 tbsp chopped fresh oregano
1 tbsp sugar
1 orange
1 oz/25 g dried porcini (cèpes) or
  other mushrooms
4 tbsp warm water
8 oz/225 g fresh plum tomatoes
cooked rice or potatoes, to serve

*This slow-cooked beef stew is
flavored with an aromatic
mixture of oranges, red wine,
and porcini (cèpes) mushrooms.*

Preheat the oven to 350°F/180°C. Heat the oil and butter in a large skillet.
Add the onions and fry over low heat, stirring occasionally, for 5 minutes,
or until golden. Remove the onions with a perforated spoon, set aside, and
keep warm.

Add the beef to the pan and cook, stirring, for 5 minutes, or until browned
all over.

Return the onions to the pan and add the stock, wine, oregano, and sugar,
stirring to mix well. Transfer the mixture to a casserole.

Pare the rind from the orange and cut it into strips. Slice the orange flesh
into rings. Add the orange rings and the rind to the casserole. Cook in the
preheated oven for 1¹/₄ hours.

Meanwhile, soak the porcini mushrooms for 30 minutes in the water.

Peel and halve the tomatoes. Add the tomatoes, porcini mushrooms, and
their soaking liquid to the casserole. Cook for an additional 20 minutes
until the beef is tender and the juices thickened. Serve the stew with
cooked rice or potatoes.

variation

*Instead of fresh tomatoes, try
using 8 sun-dried tomatoes, cut
into wide strips, if you prefer.*

michoacan beef

serves 4–6

5 minutes

about 1 hour 45 minutes

about 3 tbsp all-purpose flour
salt and pepper
2 lb 4 oz/1 kg stewing beef, cut into
   large bite-size pieces
2 tbsp vegetable oil
2 onions, chopped
5 garlic cloves, chopped
14 oz/400 g tomatoes, diced
1½ dried chipotle chiles,
   reconstituted, seeded, and cut into

thin strips, or a few shakes
   of bottled chipotle salsa
scant 1½ quarts beef stock
12 oz/350 g green beans
pinch of sugar

to serve
cooked beans
cooked rice

This rich, smoky-flavored Mexican stew is delicious; leftovers make a great filling for tacos, too!

cook's tip

This is traditionally made with nopales (edible cacti), which give the dish a distinctive flavor. Look for them in specialty stores. For this recipe you need 12–14 oz/ 350–400 g canned or fresh nopales.

Put the flour into a large bowl and season to taste with salt and pepper. Add the beef and toss to coat well. Remove the beef from the bowl, shaking off the excess flour.

Heat the oil in a skillet and brown the meat briefly over high heat. Reduce the heat to medium, add the chopped onions and garlic, and cook for 2 minutes.

Add the tomatoes, chiles, and stock, cover, and simmer over low heat for 1½ hours, or until the meat is very tender, adding the green beans and sugar 15 minutes before the end of the cooking time. Skim off any fat that rises to the surface.

Transfer to individual bowls and serve with beans and rice.

daube of beef

serves 6

5–10 minutes,
plus 8 hours marinating

about 3 hours 10 minutes

1½ cups dry white wine

2 tbsp brandy

1 tbsp white wine vinegar

4 shallots, sliced

4 carrots, sliced

1 garlic clove, finely chopped

6 black peppercorns

4 fresh thyme sprigs

1 fresh rosemary sprig

2 fresh parsley sprigs, plus
    extra to garnish

1 bay leaf

salt

1 lb 10 oz/750 g boneless rump
    roast, cut into 1-inch/2.5-cm cubes

2 tbsp olive oil

1 lb 12 oz/800 g canned
    chopped tomatoes

8 oz/225 g mushrooms, sliced

1 finely pared orange rind strip

2 oz/55 g Bayonne ham or other air-
    dried ham, cut into strips

12 black olives

mashed potatoes, to serve

A daube is a traditional French dish, in which meat was braised in a single piece, usually in wine. Once, it was cooked in a special pot placed over an open fire. Hot charcoal could be placed in the lid, so that the stew was cooked from both ends. Nowadays, an oven is easier and the meat is usually cut into cubes.

Combine the wine, brandy, vinegar, shallots, carrots, garlic, peppercorns, thyme, rosemary, parsley, and bay leaf and season to taste with salt. Add the beef, stirring to coat, then cover with plastic wrap and let stand in the refrigerator to marinate for 8 hours, or overnight.

Preheat the oven to 300°F/150°C. Drain the beef, reserving the marinade, and pat dry on paper towels. Heat half the oil in a large, flameproof casserole. Add the beef in batches and cook over medium heat, stirring, for 3–4 minutes, or until browned all over. Transfer the beef to a plate with a perforated spoon. Brown the remaining beef, adding more oil, if necessary.

Return all of the beef to the casserole and add the tomatoes and their juice, mushrooms, and orange rind. Strain the reserved marinade into the casserole. Bring to a boil, cover, and cook in the preheated oven for 2½ hours.

Remove the casserole from the oven, add the ham and olives, and return it to the oven to cook for an additional 30 minutes, or until the beef is very tender. Discard the orange rind and serve straight from the casserole, garnished with parsley, with mashed potatoes.

beef stroganoff

serves 4

10 minutes,
plus 20 minutes soaking

about 25 minutes

½ oz/15 g dried porcini
mushrooms (cèpes)
12 oz/350 g beef tenderloin
2 tbsp olive oil
4 oz/115 g shallots, sliced
6 oz/175 g fresh cremini or
portabello mushrooms

salt and pepper
½ tsp Dijon mustard
5 tbsp heavy cream
fresh chives, to garnish
freshly cooked pasta, to serve

*This traditional Slavic recipe
makes a comforting meal on a
chilly evening. Thin, delicately
cooked beef and a mustard
and cream sauce make this
straightforward dish taste out-
of-the-ordinary.*

cook's tip

*Porcini, also known as cèpes, are
widely available from large
supermarkets and delis.
You could use other dried exotic
mushrooms instead, if you prefer.*

Put the dried porcini mushrooms into a bowl and cover with hot water.
Leave to soak for 20 minutes. Meanwhile, cut the beef against the grain
into ¼-inch/5-mm thick slices, then into ½-inch/1-cm long strips and
reserve.

Drain the mushrooms, reserving the soaking liquid, and chop. Strain the
soaking liquid through a fine-mesh strainer or coffee filter paper and
reserve.

Heat half the oil in a skillet. Add the shallots and cook over low heat,
stirring occasionally, for 5 minutes, or until softened. Add the dried
mushrooms, reserved soaking water, and whole fresh mushrooms and
cook, stirring frequently, for 10 minutes, or until almost all of the liquid has
evaporated, then transfer the mixture to a plate.

Heat the remaining oil in the pan, add the beef, and cook, stirring
frequently, for 4 minutes, or until browned all over. You may need to do
this in batches. Return the mushroom mixture to the pan and season to
taste with salt and pepper. Put the mustard and cream into a small bowl
and stir to mix, then fold into the mixture. Heat through gently, then serve
with freshly cooked pasta, garnished with chives.

beef cooked in
whole spices

serves 4

5 minutes

about 1 hour 15 minutes

1¼ cups oil
3 medium onions, finely chopped
1-inch/2.5-cm piece fresh gingerroot, shredded
4 garlic cloves, shredded
2 cinnamon sticks
3 green cardamoms
3 cloves

4 black peppercorns
6 dried red chiles
²⁄₃ cup plain yogurt
1 lb/450 g lean beef, cubed
3 fresh green chiles, chopped
2½ cups water
chopped fresh cilantro, to garnish

This is a delicious way of cooking beef. The fragrant whole spices perfectly complement the meat.

Heat the oil in a skillet and fry the onions, stirring, until golden brown.

Reduce the heat and add the gingerroot, garlic, cinnamon sticks, green cardamoms, cloves, black peppercorns, and red chiles to the pan and stir-fry for 5 minutes.

In a bowl, whisk the yogurt with a fork. Add the yogurt to the onions and stir to combine.

Add the meat and 2 of the green chiles to the pan and stir-fry the mixture for 5–7 minutes.

Gradually add the water to the pan, stirring well. Cover the pan and cook the beef and spice mixture for 1 hour, stirring and adding a little more water if necessary.

When thoroughly cooked through, remove the pan from the heat and transfer the beef and spice mixture to a serving dish. Garnish with the remaining chopped green chile and the fresh cilantro.

variation

Substitute lamb for the beef in this recipe, if you prefer.

beef & orange curry

serves 4

15 minutes

1 hour 15 minutes

1 tbsp vegetable oil
8 oz/225 g shallots, halved
2 garlic cloves, crushed
1 lb/450 g lean rump or sirloin, trimmed and cut into 3/4-inch/ 2-cm cubes
3 tbsp curry paste
generous 1 3/4 cups beef stock
4 medium oranges
2 tsp cornstarch

salt and pepper
2 tbsp chopped fresh cilantro, to garnish
boiled basmati rice, to serve

raita

1/2 cucumber, finely diced
3 tbsp chopped fresh mint
2/3 cup lowfat plain yogurt
salt and pepper

A spicy blend of tender chunks of succulent beef with the tang of orange and the warmth of Indian spices.

Heat the oil in a large pan. Add the shallots, garlic, and beef cubes and cook over low heat, stirring occasionally, for 5 minutes until the beef is evenly browned all over.

Blend together the curry paste and stock. Add the mixture to the beef and stir to mix thoroughly. Bring to a boil, cover, and simmer the beef for about 1 hour.

Grate the rind of 1 orange. Squeeze the juice from the orange and from 1 other. Peel the other 2 oranges, removing the pith. Slice between each segment and remove the flesh.

Blend the cornstarch with the orange juice. At the end of the cooking time, stir the orange rind into the beef with the orange and cornstarch mixture. Bring to a boil and simmer, stirring constantly, for 3–4 minutes, or until the sauce thickens. Season to taste with salt and pepper and stir the orange segments into the curry.

To make the raita, mix the cucumber with the mint and stir in the yogurt. Season to taste with salt and pepper.

Serve the curry with rice and the cucumber raita, garnished with the chopped cilantro.

french country casserole

serves 6

15 minutes

2 hours 15 minutes

2 tbsp corn oil
4 lb 8 oz/2 kg boneless leg of lamb,
   cut into 2.5-cm/1-inch cubes
6 leeks, sliced
1 tbsp all-purpose flour
2/3 cup rosé wine
1 1/4 cups chicken stock
1 tbsp tomato paste

1 tbsp sugar
2 tbsp chopped fresh mint
4 oz/115 g dried apricots, chopped
salt and pepper
2 lb 4 oz/1 kg potatoes, sliced
3 tbsp melted unsalted butter
fresh mint sprigs, to garnish

*A crispy potato topping covers
a dish of succulent, tender lamb,
flavored with mint, leeks, and
apricots, in this traditional rustic
casserole—which tastes as good
as it looks.*

Preheat the oven to 350°F/180°C. Heat the oil in a large, flameproof casserole. Add the lamb in batches and cook over medium heat, stirring, for 5–8 minutes, or until browned. Transfer to a plate.

Add the sliced leeks to the casserole and cook, stirring occasionally, for 5 minutes, or until softened. Sprinkle in the flour and cook, stirring, for 1 minute. Pour in the wine and stock and bring to a boil, stirring. Stir in the tomato paste, sugar, chopped mint, and apricots and season to taste with salt and pepper.

Return the lamb to the casserole and stir. Arrange the potato slices on top and brush with the melted butter. Cover and cook in the preheated oven for 1 1/2 hours.

Increase the oven temperature to 400°F/200°C, uncover the casserole, and bake for an additional 30 minutes, or until the topping is golden brown. Serve immediately, garnished with fresh mint sprigs.

cook's tip

*It is always a good idea to fry off
meat to brown it before adding it to a
casserole. This will ensure that it has an
appetizing color in the finished dish.*

variation

*Use a light red wine instead of rosé
if you would prefer a slightly heavier
flavor in this country casserole.*

irish stew

serves 4

5 minutes

2 hours 30 minutes

4 tbsp all-purpose flour

salt and pepper

3 lb/1.3 kg middle neck of lamb, trimmed of visible fat

3 large onions, chopped

3 carrots, sliced

1 lb/450 g potatoes, quartered

1/2 tsp dried thyme

3 1/2 cups hot beef stock

2 tbsp chopped fresh parsley, to garnish

Nothing could be simpler, tastier, or more economical than this traditional, heart-warming stew. Serve with fresh soda bread for an authentic touch—and to mop up the delicious juices.

cook's tip

This stew is even more substantial and flavorsome if it is served with Herb Dumplings (see page 48). Add them to the casserole 30 minutes before the end of the cooking time.

Preheat the oven to 325°F/160°C. Spread the flour on a plate and season with salt and pepper. Roll the pieces of lamb in the flour to coat, shaking off any excess, and arrange in the bottom of a casserole.

Layer the onions, carrots, and potatoes on top of the lamb.

Sprinkle in the thyme and pour in the stock, then cover and cook in the preheated oven for 2 1/2 hours. Garnish with the chopped fresh parsley and serve straight from the casserole.

moroccan lamb

serves 4

10 minutes

1 hour 35 minutes

1 lb 2 oz/500 g boneless leg of lamb
1 tbsp corn oil
12 oz/350 g shallots, peeled
    but left whole
generous 1¾ cups chicken stock
1 tbsp clear honey
1 tsp ground cinnamon
½ tsp ground ginger

½ tsp saffron strands, lightly crushed
¼ tsp freshly grated nutmeg
salt and pepper
grated rind and juice of 1 small
    orange, plus extra rind to garnish
12 no-soak prunes
couscous, to serve

Slow-cooking lamb with dried fruits and spices is traditional in North Africa. Stews flavored with dried fruits, including apricots and prunes, have now become familiar elsewhere.

cook's tip

Moist "no-soak" dried fruits are available in bags in most supermarkets.

Cut the lamb into large cubes. Heat the oil in a flameproof casserole, add the lamb, and cook over medium heat, stirring, for 3–5 minutes, or until browned. Transfer to a plate. Add the shallots to the casserole and cook over low heat, stirring occasionally, for 10 minutes, or until golden. Transfer them to a separate plate with a perforated spoon.

Pour away any excess fat from the casserole, then add the stock and bring to a boil, stirring constantly and scraping up any sediment from the bottom. Return the lamb to the casserole and stir in the honey, cinnamon, ginger, saffron, and nutmeg. Season to taste with salt and pepper, cover, and simmer for 30 minutes.

Return the shallots to the casserole and add the orange rind and juice. Re-cover and simmer for an additional 30 minutes. Add the prunes and taste and adjust the seasoning, if necessary. Simmer, uncovered, for an additional 15 minutes. Garnish with orange rind and serve with couscous.

turkish lamb stew

serves 2

20 minutes

1 hour 15 minutes

12 oz/350 g lean boneless lamb

1 large or 2 small onions

1 garlic clove, crushed

½ red, yellow, or green bell pepper, coarsely diced

1¼ cups stock

1 tbsp balsamic vinegar

2 tomatoes, peeled and coarsely chopped

1½ tsp tomato paste

1 bay leaf

½ tsp dried sage

½ tsp dried dill

salt and pepper

12 oz/350 g potatoes

6–8 black olives, halved and pitted

crusty bread, to serve

A delicious blend of flavors with lamb, onions, and tomatoes, complete with potatoes makes this the perfect one-pot dish for two.

cook's tip

A good accompaniment would be a salad made of shredded white cabbage, Boston lettuce, coarsely grated carrot, diced avocado or cucumber, and scallions.

Cut the lamb into ¾-inch/2-cm cubes, discarding any excess fat or gristle.

Put into a nonstick skillet with no extra fat and heat gently until the fat runs and the meat begins to seal.

Cut the onion into 8 wedges. Add to the lamb with the garlic and fry for an additional 3–4 minutes.

Add the bell pepper, stock, vinegar, tomatoes, tomato paste, bay leaf, sage, and dill and season to taste with salt and pepper. Cover and simmer gently for 30 minutes.

Peel the potatoes and cut into ¾-inch/2-cm cubes. Add to the stew and stir well. If necessary, add a little more boiling stock or water if it seems a little dry. Re-cover the pan and simmer for an additional 25–30 minutes, or until tender.

Stir in the olives and adjust the seasoning. Simmer for an additional 5 minutes and serve with crusty bread.

lime & coconut lamb

serves 4

10 minutes

15 minutes

1 lb/450 g lean boneless lamb
2 oz/55 g creamed coconut
1¼ cups boiling water
2 tsp peanut or corn oil
1–2 garlic cloves, finely chopped
2 tsp grated fresh gingerroot

2 tbsp Thai green curry paste
grated rind and juice of 1 lime
salt and pepper
2 tbsp chopped fresh cilantro,
   plus extra to garnish
freshly cooked rice, to serve

This Thai-style curry is so delicious and tastes so authentic that your family will think you have spent hours preparing it. Only you will know just how speedy and simple it is.

cook's tip

Good-quality, ready-made Thai curry pastes are available in large supermarkets and specialty food stores, and add an authentic flavor to home-cooked Thai dishes.

Cut the lamb across the grain into strips about 1½ inches/4 cm long. Combine the creamed coconut and boiling water in a pitcher, stirring well to mix.

Heat the oil in a preheated wok or large skillet. Add the lamb, garlic, and gingerroot and fry over high heat for 2–3 minutes. Stir in the curry paste and coconut mixture and add the lime rind and juice. Season to taste with salt and pepper.

Bring the mixture to a boil, stirring constantly, then reduce the heat and simmer for 5 minutes. Stir in the chopped cilantro and serve with rice, sprinkled with extra chopped cilantro.

five-spice lamb

serves 4

10–15 minutes

15–20 minutes

1 lb 7 oz/650 g lean boneless lamb

2 tbsp peanut or corn oil

1 onion, finely chopped

1 garlic clove, finely chopped

1 red bell pepper, seeded and thinly sliced

1 yellow bell pepper, seeded and thinly sliced

2 tsp grated fresh gingerroot

6 oz/175 g green beans, halved

1 tsp Chinese five-spice powder

1 tbsp hoisin sauce

1 tbsp dark soy sauce

4 tbsp Chinese rice wine or dry sherry

to garnish

2 tbsp chopped fresh cilantro

1 tbsp toasted sesame seeds

Chinese five-spice powder, ginger, and soy and hoisin sauces flavor this quick and easy aromatic stir-fry—an unusual, Eastern-style dish, which is a great idea for impressing guests.

Cut the lamb across the grain into strips about 1 1/2 inches/4 cm long. Heat the oil in a preheated wok or large skillet. Add the lamb and stir-fry over high heat for 4 minutes, or until browned all over. Transfer to a plate with a perforated spoon.

Add the onion, garlic, bell peppers, and gingerroot to the wok and stir-fry for 3–4 minutes. Add the beans and stir-fry for an additional 2 minutes.

Return the lamb to the wok, then stir in the Chinese five-spice powder, hoisin sauce, soy sauce, and Chinese rice wine or sherry. Cook, stirring and tossing the mixture constantly, until the lamb is tender and coated in the sauce. Serve, garnished with chopped cilantro and toasted sesame seeds.

cook's tip

Chinese five-spice powder and rice wine are available from large supermarkets and specialty food stores. Note that the Chinese spice is different from Indian five-spice powder.

variation

To add some spiciness, add 1–2 fresh red chiles, seeded and chopped, with the bell peppers and ginger. Serve this dish with freshly cooked rice or egg noodles.

lamb hotchpotch

serves 4

10–15 minutes

2 hours

1 ½ lb/675 g lean lamb neck slices
2 lamb's kidneys
1 ½ lb/675 g waxy potatoes, scrubbed and thinly sliced
1 large onion, thinly sliced

2 tbsp chopped fresh thyme
⅔ cup lamb stock
salt and pepper
2 tbsp butter, melted
fresh thyme sprigs, to garnish

This classic recipe using lamb neck slices layered between sliced potatoes, kidneys, onions, and herbs makes a perfect meal on a cold winter's day.

variation

Traditionally, oysters are also included in this hotchpotch. Add them to the layers along with the kidneys, if wished.

Preheat the oven to 350°F/180°C. Remove any excess fat from the lamb. Skin and core the kidneys and cut them into slices.

Arrange a layer of potatoes in the bottom of a 1½-quart ovenproof dish.

Arrange the lamb neck slices on top of the potatoes and cover with the sliced kidneys, onion, and chopped thyme.

Pour the stock over the meat and season to taste with salt and pepper. Layer the remaining potato slices on top, overlapping to completely cover the meat and sliced onion.

Brush the potato slices with the butter, cover the dish, and cook in the preheated oven for 1½ hours.

Remove the lid and cook for an additional 30 minutes until golden brown on top. Garnish with fresh thyme sprigs and serve hot.

lamb biryani

serves 4–6

5 minutes

about 1 hour 45 minutes

2/3 cup milk

1 tsp saffron

5 tbsp pure or vegetable ghee, or vegetable oil

3 onions, sliced

2 lb 4 oz/1 kg lean lamb, cubed

7 tbsp plain yogurt

1–2 garlic cloves, crushed

1 1/2 tsp finely chopped fresh gingerroot

2 tsp garam masala

2 tsp salt

1/4 tsp ground turmeric

2 1/2 cups water

1 lb/450 g basmati rice

2 tsp black cumin seeds

3 green cardamoms

4 tbsp lemon juice

2 fresh green chiles

1/4 bunch fresh cilantro

Cooked on festive occasions, especially for weddings, lamb biryani is one of the most popular dishes in India. The meat can be cooked in advance and added to the rice on the day of the party.

Boil the milk in a pan with the saffron and set aside. Heat the ghee or oil in a pan and fry the onions until golden. Remove half of the onions and ghee or oil from the pan and set aside in a bowl.

Combine the lamb, yogurt, garlic, gingerroot, garam masala, 1 tsp of the salt, and turmeric in a large bowl and mix well.

Return the pan with the ghee or oil and onions to the heat, add the lamb mixture, stir for about 3 minutes, and add the water. Cook over low heat for 45 minutes, stirring occasionally. Check to see whether the meat is tender: if not, add 2/3 cup water and cook for 15 minutes. Once all the water has evaporated, stir-fry for about 2 minutes and set aside.

Meanwhile, put the rice into a pan. Add the cumin, cardamoms, remaining salt, and enough water for cooking and cook over medium heat until the rice is half-cooked. Drain. Remove half of the rice and put into a bowl.

Spoon the lamb mixture on top of the rice in the pan. Add half each of the saffron mixture, lemon juice, chiles, and cilantro. Add the other half of the rice, saffron, lemon juice, chiles, and cilantro. Cover and cook over low heat for 15–20 minutes, or until the rice is cooked. Stir well, add the remaining fried onions, and serve hot.

spicy pork with prunes

serves 4–6

5 minutes,
plus 8 hours marinating

3–4 hours

juice of 2–3 limes
10 garlic cloves, chopped
3–4 tbsp mild chili powder
4 tbsp vegetable oil
salt
1 pork joint, such as leg or shoulder,
  weighing about 3 lb 5 oz/1.5 kg
2 onions, chopped
generous 2 cups chicken stock

25 small tomatoes, coarsely chopped
25 prunes, pitted
1–2 tsp sugar
pinch of ground cinnamon
pinch of allspice
pinch of ground cumin
pinch of chili powder (optional)
warmed corn tortillas, to serve

Prunes add an earthy, wine flavor to this spicy stew. Serve with tortillas or crusty bread to dip into the rich sauce.

Mix the lime juice, garlic, chili powder, 2 tablespoons of the oil, and salt together and rub all over the pork. Let stand in the refrigerator to marinate overnight.

Preheat the oven to 350°F/180°C. Remove the pork from the marinade. Wipe the pork dry with paper towels and reserve the marinade. Heat the remaining oil in a flameproof casserole and brown the pork evenly until just golden. Add the onions, the reserved marinade, and stock. Cover and cook in the preheated oven for 2–3 hours, or until tender.

Spoon off fat from the surface of the cooking liquid and add the tomatoes. Continue to cook for 20 minutes, or until the tomatoes are tender. Mash the tomatoes into a coarse purée. Add the prunes and sugar, then adjust the seasoning, adding cinnamon, allspice, and cumin to taste, as well as chili powder, if using.

Increase the oven temperature to 400°F/200°C and return the meat and sauce to the oven for an additional 20–30 minutes, or until the meat has browned on top and the juices have thickened.

Remove the meat from the casserole and set aside for a few minutes. Carefully carve it into thin slices and spoon the sauce over the top. Serve warm with corn tortillas.

country pork with onions

serves 4

about 30 minutes

4 hours 15 minutes

2 large pork hocks
2 large garlic cloves, sliced
3 tbsp olive oil
2 carrots, finely chopped
2 celery stalks, finely chopped
1 large onion, finely chopped
2 fresh thyme sprigs, broken
   into pieces
2 fresh rosemary sprigs, broken
   into pieces

1 large bay leaf
1 cup dry white wine
1 cup water
salt and pepper
20 pickling onions
coarsely chopped fresh flatleaf
   parsley, to garnish

This rustic Mediterranean stew makes the most of inexpensive cuts that require slow cooking and robust flavoring.

Preheat the oven to 325°F/160°C. Using the tip of a sharp knife, make slits all over the pork and insert the garlic slices.

Heat 1 tablespoon of the oil in a flameproof casserole over medium heat. Add the carrots, celery, and onion and cook, stirring occasionally, for 10 minutes, or until softened.

Place the pork on top of the vegetables. Sprinkle the thyme and rosemary over the meat. Add the bay leaf, wine, and water and season with pepper.

Bring to a boil, then remove the casserole from the heat. Cover tightly and cook in the preheated oven for 3½ hours, or until the meat is very tender.

Meanwhile, put the onions into a bowl, pour over boiling water to cover, and set aside for 1 minute. Drain, then slip off all the skins. Heat the remaining oil in a large, heavy-bottomed skillet. Add the onions, partially cover, and cook over low heat for 15 minutes, shaking the pan occasionally, until the onions are just starting to turn golden.

When the pork is tender, add the onions to the casserole and return to the oven for an additional 15 minutes. Remove the pork and onions from the casserole and keep warm.

Using a large metal spoon, skim off as much fat as possible from the surface of the cooking liquid. Strain the liquid into a bowl, pressing down to extract the flavor; reserve the strained vegetables. Adjust the seasoning.

Cut the pork from the bones, if wished. Arrange on a serving platter with the onions and vegetables. Spoon over the sauce. Garnish with parsley.

basque pork & beans

serves 4–6

35 minutes,
plus 8 hours soaking

1 hour 45 minutes

1 cup dried cannellini beans, soaked
   in cold water overnight
olive oil, for frying
1 lb 5 oz/600 g boneless leg of pork,
   cut into 2-inch/5-cm chunks
1 large onion, sliced
3 large garlic cloves, crushed

14 oz/400 g canned
   chopped tomatoes
2 green bell peppers, seeded
   and sliced
finely grated rind of 1 large orange
salt and pepper
finely chopped fresh parsley,
   to garnish

*Dried cannellini beans feature in
many Italian, Spanish, French, and
Greek stews and casseroles,
especially during the winter.*

variation

*Any leftover beans and bell
peppers can be used as a pasta
sauce. Add sliced and fried
chorizo sausage for
a spicier dish.*

Drain the cannellini beans and put into a large pan with fresh water to
cover. Bring to a boil and boil rapidly for 10 minutes. Reduce the heat and
simmer for 20 minutes. Drain and set aside.

Preheat the oven to 350°F/180°C. Add enough oil to cover the bottom of
a skillet in a very thin layer. Heat the oil over medium heat, add a few
pieces of the pork, and fry on all sides until brown. Remove from the pan
and set aside. Repeat with the remaining pork.

Add 1 tablespoon oil to the pan, if necessary, then add the onion and cook
for 3 minutes. Stir in the garlic and cook for an additional 2 minutes.
Return the pork to the pan.

Add the tomatoes and bring to a boil. Reduce the heat and stir in the bell
pepper slices, orange rind, and the drained cannellini beans. Season to
taste with salt and pepper.

Transfer the contents of the pan to a casserole. Cover the casserole and
cook in the preheated oven for 45 minutes, or until the beans and pork
are tender. Sprinkle with chopped parsley and serve immediately, straight
from the casserole.

pork hotchpotch

serves 6

5–10 minutes

1 hour 20 minutes

generous ½ cup all-purpose flour

salt and pepper

3 lb/1.3 kg pork tenderloin, cut into ¼-inch/5-mm slices

4 tbsp corn oil

2 onions, thinly sliced

2 garlic cloves

14 oz/400 g canned chopped tomatoes

1½ cups dry white wine

1 tbsp torn fresh basil leaves

2 tbsp chopped fresh parsley

fresh parsley sprigs, to garnish

fresh crusty bread, to serve

This tasty pork and tomato hotchpotch requires nothing more than plenty of fresh crusty bread to mop up the delicious juices, but you could also serve it with a fresh green salad.

variation

Substitute 6 peeled, seeded, and chopped fresh tomatoes for the canned ones, adding them with the wine.

Spread the flour on a plate and season with salt and pepper. Coat the pork slices in the flour, shaking off any excess. Heat the oil in a flameproof casserole. Add the pork slices and cook over medium heat, turning occasionally, for 4–5 minutes, or until browned all over. Transfer the pork to a plate with a perforated spoon.

Add the onion slices to the casserole and cook over low heat, stirring occasionally, for 10 minutes, or until golden brown. Finely chop the garlic, add it to the casserole, and cook for an additional 2 minutes, then add the tomatoes, wine, and basil leaves and season to taste with salt and pepper. Cook, stirring frequently, for 3 minutes.

Return the pork to the casserole, cover, and simmer gently for 1 hour, or until the meat is tender. Sprinkle over the chopped parsley, garnish with parsley sprigs, and serve immediately with fresh crusty bread.

pork & sausage bake

serves 4

15 minutes

about 1 hour 25 minutes

2 tbsp corn oil
2 tbsp butter
1 lb/450 g pork loin,
    cut into thin strips
1 large onion, chopped
1 red bell pepper, seeded and sliced
1 orange bell pepper, seeded and
    sliced

4 oz/115 g mushrooms, sliced
2/3 cup long-grain rice
generous 1 3/4 cups beef stock
8 oz/225 g smoked sausage, sliced
1/4 tsp allspice
salt and pepper
2 tbsp chopped fresh parsley,
    to garnish

This would be a lovely treat for a midweek family supper, and you can take time to relax while it's cooking. It is substantial enough to satisfy even the heartiest appetite.

Preheat the oven to 350°F/180°C. Heat the oil and butter in a large, flameproof casserole. Add the pork and cook over medium heat, stirring, for 5 minutes until browned. Transfer to a plate.

Add the onion and cook over low heat, stirring occasionally, for 5 minutes, or until softened. Add the bell peppers and cook, stirring frequently, for an additional 4–5 minutes. Add the mushrooms and cook for 1 minute, then stir in the rice. Cook for 1 minute, or until the grains are well coated, then add the stock and bring to a boil.

Return the pork to the casserole, add the sausage and allspice, and season to taste with salt and pepper. Mix thoroughly, cover, and cook in the pre-heated oven for 1 hour, or until all the liquid has been absorbed and the meat is tender. Serve immediately, garnished with chopped parsley.

cook's tip

A huge variety of smoked sausages are available, from pepperoni and many types of salami to saucisson fumé aux herbes, with a herb coating.

variation

You can use unsmoked sausages for this casserole, but you should brown them with the pork before adding the onion.

italian sausage & bean
casserole

serves 4

5 minutes

about 30 minutes

1 green bell pepper
8 Italian sausages
1 tbsp olive oil
1 large onion, chopped
2 garlic cloves, chopped

8oz/225 g fresh tomatoes, peeled
 and chopped, or 14 oz/400 g
 canned tomatoes, chopped
2 tbsp sun-dried tomato paste
14 oz/400 g canned cannellini beans,
 drained and rinsed
mashed potatoes or boiled rice,
 to serve

*In this traditional Tuscan dish,
Italian sausages are cooked with
cannellini beans and tomatoes.*

cook's tip

*Italian sausages are coarse
in texture and have quite a
strong flavor. They can be
found in specialty stores, Italian
delis, and some larger
supermarkets. Game sausages
can be substituted for the
Italian sausages.*

Seed the bell pepper and cut it into thin strips.

Prick the Italian sausages all over with a fork. Cook under a preheated broiler, turning occasionally, for 10–12 minutes, or until brown all over. Set aside and keep warm.

Heat the oil in a large skillet. Add the onion, garlic, and bell pepper to the pan and cook, stirring occasionally, for 5 minutes, or until softened.

Add the chopped tomatoes to the pan and let the mixture simmer, stirring occasionally, for 5 minutes, or until slightly reduced and thickened.

Stir the sun-dried tomato paste, cannellini beans, and Italian sausages into the mixture. Cook for 4–5 minutes, or until the mixture is piping hot. Add 4–5 tablespoons of water if the mixture becomes too dry during cooking.

Transfer the casserole to serving plates and serve with mashed potatoes or cooked rice.

osso bucco with
citrus rinds

serves 6

5 minutes

1 hour 35 minutes

1–2 tbsp all-purpose flour

salt and pepper

6 meaty slices veal shank

2 lb 4 oz/1 kg fresh tomatoes, peeled, seeded, and diced, or 1 lb 12oz/ 800 g canned chopped tomatoes

1–2 tbsp olive oil

9 oz/250 g onions, very finely chopped

9 oz/250 g carrots, finely diced

1 cup dry white wine

1 cup veal stock

6 large basil leaves, torn

1 large garlic clove, very finely chopped

finely grated rind of 1 large lemon

finely grated rind of 1 orange

2 tbsp finely chopped fresh flatleaf parsley

The orange and lemon rinds, together with fresh basil, give this traditional Italian dish a real southern flavor.

Put the flour into a plastic bag and season with salt and pepper. Add the veal, a few pieces at a time, and shake until well coated. Remove and shake off the excess flour.

If using canned tomatoes, put into a nonmetallic strainer and let drain.

Heat 1 tablespoon of the oil in a large flameproof casserole. Add the veal and fry for 10 minutes on each side until well browned. Remove from the casserole.

Add 1–2 teaspoons more oil to the casserole, if necessary. Add the onions and cook, stirring constantly, for 5 minutes, or until soft. Stir in the carrots and cook until softened.

Add the tomatoes, wine, stock, and basil and return the veal to the casserole. Bring to a boil, then reduce the heat, cover, and simmer for 1 hour. Check that the meat is tender with the tip of a knife. If not, continue cooking for 10 minutes and test again.

When the meat is tender, sprinkle with the garlic and lemon and orange rinds, re-cover, and cook over low heat for an additional 10 minutes.

Taste and adjust the seasoning if necessary. Sprinkle with the parsley and serve immediately.

brittany chicken casserole

serves 6

8 hours soaking

2 hours 50 minutes

1 lb 2 oz/500 g dried beans, such as flageolets, soaked overnight and drained
2 tbsp butter
2 tbsp olive oil
3 rindless bacon slices, chopped
2 lb/900 g chicken pieces
1 tbsp all-purpose flour

1¼ cups hard cider
⅔ cup chicken stock
salt and pepper
14 shallots
2 tbsp clear honey, warmed
9 oz/250 g ready-cooked beets

A hearty, one-dish meal that would make a substantial lunch or supper. As it requires a long cooking time, make double quantities and freeze half to eat later.

cook's tip

To save time, use canned flageolet beans instead of dried. Drain and rinse before adding to the chicken.

Cook the beans in a large pan of boiling water for about 25 minutes.

Preheat the oven to 325°F/160°C. Heat the butter and oil in a flameproof casserole, add the bacon and chicken, and cook for 5 minutes.

Sprinkle with the flour, then add the hard cider and stock, stirring constantly to avoid lumps forming. Season to taste with salt and pepper and bring to a boil.

Add the beans, then cover the casserole tightly with a lid or foil and bake in the center of the preheated oven for 2 hours.

About 15 minutes before the end of cooking time, remove the lid or foil from the casserole.

In a skillet, gently cook the shallots and honey together for 5 minutes, turning the shallots frequently.

Add the shallots and cooked beets to the casserole and let finish cooking in the oven for the last 15 minutes.

casserole chicken with olives & thyme

serves 4

5 minutes

1 hour 20 minutes

8 chicken thighs

2 tbsp olive oil

1 red onion, sliced

2 garlic cloves, crushed

1 large red bell pepper, thickly sliced

thinly pared rind and juice of 1 small orange

½ cup chicken stock

14 oz/400 g canned chopped tomatoes

1 oz/25 g sun-dried tomatoes, thinly sliced

1 tbsp chopped fresh thyme

⅓ cup pitted black olives

salt and pepper

fresh thyme sprigs and orange rind strips, to garnish

crusty fresh bread, to serve

A colorful casserole packed with sunshine flavors from the Mediterranean. Sun-dried tomatoes add a wonderful richness and you need very few to make this dish really special.

In a heavy-bottomed or nonstick large skillet, fry the chicken without fat over fairly high heat, turning occasionally, until golden brown. Using a perforated spoon, drain off any excess fat from the chicken and transfer to a flameproof casserole.

Fry the onion, garlic, and bell pepper in the skillet over medium heat for 3–4 minutes. Transfer to the casserole.

Add the orange rind and juice, stock, canned tomatoes, and sun-dried tomatoes and stir to combine.

Bring to a boil, then cover the casserole with a lid and simmer very gently over low heat for about 1 hour, stirring occasionally. Add the chopped fresh thyme and pitted black olives and season to taste with salt and pepper.

Scatter thyme sprigs and orange rind strips over the casserole to garnish and serve with crusty bread.

garlic chicken casserole

serves 4

5 minutes

2 hours 25 minutes

4 tbsp corn oil

2 lb/900 g skinless, boneless chicken, chopped

9 oz/250 g mushrooms, sliced

16 shallots

6 garlic cloves, crushed

1 tbsp all-purpose flour

generous 1 cup white wine

generous 1 cup chicken stock

1 bouquet garni (1 bay leaf, 1 sprig each fresh thyme, parsley, and sage, and ½ celery stalk, tied together with string)

salt and pepper

14 oz/400 g canned cranberry or cannellini beans, drained and rinsed

small squash, to serve

This is a cassoulet with a twist—it is made with chicken instead of duck and lamb. Save time by using canned beans, such as cranberry or cannellini beans, which are both good in this dish.

cook's tip

Mushrooms are high in flavor and contain no fat. Experiment with the wealth of varieties that are now available from supermarkets.

Serve the casserole with brown rice to make this filling dish go even further.

Preheat the oven to 300°F/150°C. Heat the oil in an ovenproof casserole and fry the chicken pieces until browned all over. Remove the chicken from the casserole with a perforated spoon and set aside until required.

Add the mushrooms, shallots, and garlic to the casserole and cook for 4 minutes.

Return the chicken to the casserole and sprinkle with the flour, then cook for an additional 2 minutes.

Add the wine and stock, stir until boiling, then add the bouquet garni. Season well with salt and pepper.

Add the beans to the casserole. Cover and cook in the center of the preheated oven for 2 hours. Remove and discard the bouquet garni and serve the casserole with small squash.

country chicken bake

serves 4

5 minutes

1 hour 5 minutes

2 tbsp corn oil

4 chicken quarters

16 small whole onions, peeled

3 celery stalks, sliced

14 oz/400 g canned red kidney beans

4 tomatoes, quartered

generous 3/4 cup dry hard cider or stock

4 tbsp chopped fresh parsley

salt and pepper

1 tsp paprika

2 tbsp butter

12 slices French bread

This economical bake is a complete meal—its crusty, herb-flavored French bread topping mops up the tasty juices, and means there's no need to serve potatoes or rice separately.

Preheat the oven to 400°F/200°C. Heat the oil in a flameproof casserole and fry the chicken quarters 2 at a time until golden. Using a perforated spoon, remove the chicken from the casserole and set aside until required.

Add the onions and fry, turning occasionally, until golden brown. Add the celery and fry for 2–3 minutes. Return the chicken to the casserole, then stir in the beans, tomatoes, hard cider or stock, half the parsley, and salt and pepper to taste. Sprinkle with the paprika.

Cover and cook in the preheated oven for 20–25 minutes, or until the chicken juices run clear when pierced with a skewer.

Mix the remaining parsley with the butter and spread evenly over the French bread.

Uncover the casserole, arrange the bread slices overlapping on top, and bake for an additional 10–12 minutes, or until golden and crisp.

cook's tip

Add a crushed garlic clove to the parsley butter for extra flavor.

variation

For a more unusual Italian-tasting dish, replace the garlic and parsley bread topping with pesto.

springtime chicken cobbler

serves 4

about 20 minutes

I hour 40 minutes

1 tbsp vegetable oil
8 skinless chicken drumsticks
1 small onion, sliced
12 oz/350 g baby carrots
2 baby turnips
4½ oz/125 g fava beans or peas
1 tsp cornstarch
1¼ cups chicken stock
2 bay leaves
salt and pepper

cobbler topping

9 oz/250 g all-purpose whole-wheat flour
2 tsp baking powder
2 tbsp soft margarine
2 tsp dry whole-grain mustard
2 oz/55 g lowfat sharp Cheddar cheese, grated
skim milk, for mixing and brushing
sesame seeds, for sprinkling

Fresh spring vegetables are the basis of this colorful casserole, which is topped with hearty whole-wheat dumplings.

Preheat the oven to 400°F/200°C. Heat the oil in a large, heavy-bottomed skillet and fry the chicken, turning occasionally, until golden brown. Drain well and place in a casserole. Add the sliced onion to the pan and cook, stirring occasionally, for 2–3 minutes, or until softened.

Cut the carrots and turnips into equal-size pieces. Add to the casserole with the onion and fava beans or peas.

Blend the cornstarch with a little of the stock, then stir in the remainder and heat gently, stirring, until boiling. Pour into the casserole and add the bay leaves. Season to taste with salt and pepper.

Cover tightly and cook in the preheated oven for 50–60 minutes, or until the chicken is tender and the juices run clear when pierced with a skewer.

For the topping, sift the flour and baking powder into a bowl. Mix in the margarine with a fork. Stir in the mustard, cheese, and enough milk to mix to a fairly soft dough.

Roll out and cut out 16 rounds with a 1½-inch/4-cm cookie cutter. Uncover the casserole, arrange the rounds on top of the chicken, then brush with milk and sprinkle with sesame seeds. Return to the oven and cook for 20 minutes, or until the topping is golden and firm.

green chicken curry

serves 4

10 minutes

about 45 minutes

6 skinless, boneless chicken thighs
1 1/4 cups coconut milk
2 garlic cloves, crushed
2 tbsp Thai fish sauce
2 tbsp Thai green curry paste
12 baby eggplants

3 fresh green chiles, finely chopped
3 kaffir lime leaves, shredded
salt and pepper
4 tbsp chopped fresh cilantro
boiled rice, to serve

Thai curries are traditionally very hot, and designed to make a little go a long way—the thin, highly spiced juices are eaten with lots of rice to "stretch" a small amount of meat as far as possible.

cook's tip

Baby eggplants, or "pea eggplants" as they are called in Thailand, are traditionally used in this curry, but they are not always easily available outside the country. If you can't find them in a supermarket or specialty food store, use chopped ordinary eggplant or substitute a few green peas.

Cut the chicken into bite-size pieces. Pour the coconut milk into a large skillet or wok and bring to a boil over high heat.

Add the chicken, garlic, and fish sauce to the pan and return to a boil. Reduce the heat and simmer gently for 30 minutes, or until the chicken is just tender.

Remove the chicken from the mixture with a perforated spoon. Set aside and keep warm.

Stir the green curry paste into the pan, add the eggplants, chiles, and lime leaves and simmer for 5 minutes.

Return the chicken to the pan and bring to a boil. Season to taste with salt and pepper, then stir in the cilantro. Serve the curry with boiled rice.

jamaican hotchpotch

serves 4

10–15 minutes

1 hour 20 minutes

2 tsp corn oil
4 chicken drumsticks
4 chicken thighs
1 medium onion
1 lb 10 oz/750 g squash
or pumpkin
1 green bell pepper
1-inch/2.5-cm piece fresh gingerroot,
finely chopped

14 oz/400 g canned chopped
tomatoes
1 1/4 cups chicken stock
scant 1/3 cup split lentils
garlic salt
cayenne pepper
12 oz/350 g canned corn, drained
salt and pepper
crusty bread, to serve

A tasty way to make chicken pieces go a long way, this hearty casserole, spiced with the warm, subtle flavor of ginger, is a good choice for a Halloween party.

variation

If squash or pumpkin is not available, rutabaga makes a good substitute.

If you can't find fresh gingerroot, add 1 tsp allspice for a warm, fragrant aroma.

Preheat the oven to 375°F/190°C. Heat the oil in a large flameproof casserole and fry the chicken pieces until golden, turning frequently.

Using a sharp knife, peel and slice the onion, peel and dice the pumpkin or squash, and seed and slice the bell pepper.

Drain any excess fat from the casserole and add the prepared onion, pumpkin, and bell pepper. Gently fry for a few minutes until lightly browned. Add the chopped gingerroot, tomatoes, stock, and lentils. Season lightly with garlic salt and cayenne pepper.

Cover the casserole and cook in the preheated oven for 1 hour, or until the vegetables are tender and the chicken juices run clear when pierced with a skewer.

Add the drained corn and cook for an additional 5 minutes. Season to taste with salt and pepper and serve with crusty bread.

stew of meat, chicken, vegetables & fruit

serves 6–8

5 minutes

2 hours 10 minutes

2 lb/900 g boneless pork, in one
  or several pieces
2 bay leaves
1 onion, chopped
8 garlic cloves, finely chopped
2 tbsp chopped fresh cilantro
1 carrot, thinly sliced
2 celery stalks, diced
2 chicken bouillon cubes
1/2 chicken, cut into pieces
4–5 ripe tomatoes, diced
1/2 tsp mild chili powder
grated rind of 1/4 orange
1/4 tsp ground cumin

juice of 3 oranges
1 zucchini, cut into bite-size pieces
1/4 cabbage, thinly sliced and
  blanched
1 apple, cut into bite-size pieces
about 10 prunes, pitted
1/4 tsp ground cinnamon
pinch of ground ginger
2 hard chorizo sausages, about
  12 oz/350 g in total, cut into
  bite-size pieces
salt and pepper

*A big pot of this Spanish stew,
known as cocido, is warming on
a cold day, and a great choice for a
family meal. Serve with a selection
of several salsas, a stack of corn
tortillas, and a bowl of rice.*

Combine the pork, bay leaves, onion, garlic, cilantro, carrot, and celery in a
large, flameproof casserole and fill with cold water. Bring to a boil and skim
off any foam that rises to the surface. Reduce the heat and simmer gently
for 1 hour.

Add the bouillon cubes to the casserole, along with the chicken, tomatoes,
chili powder, orange rind, and cumin. Continue to cook for an additional
45 minutes, or until the chicken is tender. Spoon off the fat that forms on
the top of the liquid.

Add the orange juice, zucchini, cabbage, apple, prunes, cinnamon, ginger,
and chorizo. Continue to simmer for an additional 20 minutes, or until the
zucchini is soft and tender and the chorizo cooked through.

Season the stew to taste with salt and pepper and serve immediately.

chicken basquaise

serves 4–5

5 minutes

1 hour 20 minutes

1 chicken, weighing about 3 lb/1.3 kg, cut into 8 pieces

2 tbsp all-purpose flour, for dusting

salt and pepper

3 tbsp olive oil

1 Spanish onion, thickly sliced

2 red or yellow bell peppers, seeded and cut lengthwise into thick strips

2 garlic cloves

5 oz/140 g spicy chorizo sausage, skinned and cut into ½-inch/1-cm pieces

1 tbsp tomato paste

1 cup long-grain white rice

1¾ cups chicken stock

1 tsp dried chili flakes

½ tsp dried thyme

4 oz/115 g Bayonne or other air-dried ham, diced

12 dry-cured black olives

2 tbsp chopped fresh flatleaf parsley

Sweet bell peppers are typical of dishes from the Basque region in France. In this recipe, Bayonne ham, from the Pyrenees, adds a delicious flavor.

Wipe the chicken pieces with paper towels. Put the flour into a plastic bag, season with salt and pepper, and add the chicken pieces. Seal the bag and shake to coat the chicken.

Heat 2 tablespoons of the oil in a large, flameproof casserole over medium–high heat. Add the chicken and cook, turning frequently, for 15 minutes, or until well browned all over. Transfer to a plate.

Heat the remaining oil in the casserole and add the onion and bell peppers. Reduce the heat to medium and stir-fry until beginning to color and soften. Add the garlic, chorizo, and tomato paste and cook, stirring constantly, for about 3 minutes. Add the rice and cook, stirring to coat, for 2 minutes, or until the rice is translucent.

Add the stock, dried chili flakes, and thyme, season to taste with salt and pepper, and stir well. Bring to a boil. Return the chicken to the casserole, pressing it gently into the rice. Cover and cook the casserole over very low heat for 45 minutes, or until the chicken is cooked through and the rice is tender.

Gently stir the ham, black olives, and half the parsley into the rice mixture. Re-cover and heat through for an additional 5 minutes. Sprinkle with the remaining parsley and serve immediately.

country chicken hotchpotch

serves 4

5–10 minutes

about 2 hours

4 chicken quarters

6 potatoes, cut into ¼-inch/ 5-mm slices

salt and pepper

2 fresh thyme sprigs

2 fresh rosemary sprigs

2 bay leaves

7 oz/200 g rindless smoked bacon, diced

1 large onion, finely chopped

2 carrots, sliced

⅔ cup stout

2 tbsp melted butter

freshly cooked seasonal vegetables, to serve

There are many regional versions of hotchpotch, all using fresh, local ingredients available all year, perfect for traditional one-pot cooking.

Preheat the oven to 300°F/150°C. Remove the skin from the chicken quarters, if desired.

Arrange a layer of potato slices in the bottom of a wide casserole. Season to taste with salt and pepper, then add the thyme, rosemary, and bay leaves.

Top with the chicken quarters, then sprinkle with the diced bacon, onion, and carrots. Season well with salt and pepper and arrange the remaining potato slices on top, overlapping slightly.

Pour over the stout, brush the potatoes with the melted butter, and cover with a lid.

Cook in the preheated oven for about 2 hours, uncovering the casserole for the last 30 minutes to let the potatoes brown. Serve hot with freshly cooked seasonal vegetables.

cook's tip

Serve the hotchpotch with dumplings for a truly hearty meal.

variation

This dish is also delicious with stewing lamb, cut into chunks. You can add different vegetables depending on what is in season.

golden chicken pilau

serves 4

10 minutes

15–20 minutes

2 tbsp butter

8 skinless, boneless chicken thighs, cut into large pieces

1 onion, sliced

1 tsp ground turmeric

1 tsp ground cinnamon

1 1/4 cups long-grain rice

salt and pepper

generous 1 3/4 cups plain yogurt

generous 1/3 cup golden raisins

generous 3/4 cup chicken stock

1 tomato, chopped

2 tbsp chopped fresh cilantro or parsley

2 tbsp toasted coconut

fresh cilantro sprigs, to garnish

This is a simple version of a creamy textured and mildly spiced Indian pilau. Although there are lots of ingredients, there's very little preparation needed for this dish.

cook's tip

Long-grain rice is the cheapest and most widely available type of rice. Basmati, with its slender grains and aromatic flavor, is more expensive and should be used on special occasions if it is not affordable on a frequent basis. Rice, especially basmati, should be washed thoroughly under cold running water before use.

Heat the butter in a heavy-bottomed or nonstick skillet and fry the chicken with the onion for about 3 minutes.

Stir in the turmeric, cinnamon, and rice and season to taste with salt and pepper. Fry gently for 3 minutes.

Add the yogurt, golden raisins, and stock and mix well. Cover and simmer, stirring occasionally, for 10 minutes, or until the rice is tender and all the stock has been absorbed. Add more stock if the mixture becomes too dry.

Stir in the chopped tomato and fresh cilantro or parsley.

Sprinkle the pilau with the toasted coconut and garnish with cilantro.

chicken risotto

à la milanese

serves 4

5 minutes

about I hour

generous ½ cup butter

2 lb/900 g skinless, boneless chicken, thinly sliced

I large onion, chopped

2½ cups risotto rice

2½ cups chicken stock

⅔ cup white wine

I tsp crumbled saffron strands

salt and pepper

½ cup grated Parmesan cheese, to serve

This famous dish is known throughout the world—it is perhaps the best known of all Italian risottos, although there are many variations.

Heat 4 tablespoons of the butter in a deep skillet and cook the chicken and onion until golden brown.

Add the rice, stir well, and cook over low heat for 15 minutes.

Heat the stock until boiling and gradually add to the rice. Add the wine, saffron, and salt and pepper to taste and mix well. Simmer gently for 20 minutes, stirring occasionally and adding more stock if necessary.

Set aside for 2–3 minutes. Just before serving, add a little more stock and simmer for 10 minutes. Serve the risotto, sprinkled with the grated Parmesan cheese and the remaining butter.

cook's tip

A risotto should have moist but separate grains. Stock should be added a little at a time and only when the last addition has been completely absorbed.

variation

The possibilities for risotto are endless—try adding the following just at the end of the cooking time: cashews and corn, lightly sautéed zucchini and basil, or artichokes and mushrooms.

sage chicken & rice

serves 4

5–10 minutes

50 minutes

1 large onion, chopped
1 garlic clove, crushed
2 celery stalks, sliced
2 carrots, diced
2 fresh sage sprigs
1¼ cups chicken stock
12 oz/350 g skinless, boneless, chicken breasts
generous 1 cup mixed brown and wild rice

14 oz/400 g canned chopped tomatoes
dash of Tabasco sauce
salt and pepper
2 zucchini, thinly sliced
3½ oz/100 g cooked lean ham, diced
fresh sage leaves, to garnish
salad greens and crusty bread, to serve

Cooking in a single pot means that all of the flavors are retained. This is a substantial meal that needs only a salad and some crusty bread to accompany it.

cook's tip

If you do not have fresh sage, use 1 teaspoon dried sage instead.

Put the onion, garlic, celery, carrots, and sage sprigs into a large pan and pour in the stock. Bring to a boil, cover the pan, and simmer for 5 minutes.

Cut the chicken into 1-inch/2.5-cm cubes. Stir the cubes into the pan with the vegetables. Cover the pan and continue to cook for an additional 5 minutes.

Stir in the rice and chopped tomatoes. Add a dash of Tabasco sauce to taste and season well with salt and pepper. Bring to a boil, cover, and simmer for 25 minutes.

Stir in the sliced zucchini and diced ham and continue to cook, uncovered, for an additional 10 minutes, stirring occasionally, or until the rice is just tender.

Remove and discard the sage sprigs. Garnish with a few fresh sage leaves and serve with salad greens and crusty bread.

thai stir-fried chicken with vegetables

serves 4

15 minutes

about 10 minutes

3 tbsp sesame oil

12 oz/350 g skinless, boneless
chicken breasts, thinly sliced

salt and pepper

8 shallots, sliced

2 garlic cloves, finely chopped

2 tsp grated fresh gingerroot

1 fresh green chile, seeded and
finely chopped

1 red bell pepper, seeded and
thinly sliced

1 green bell pepper, seeded and
thinly sliced

3 zucchini, thinly sliced

2 tbsp ground almonds

1 tsp ground cinnamon

1 tbsp oyster sauce

3/4 oz/20 g creamed coconut, grated

*Coconut adds a creamy texture
and delicious flavor to this Thai-
style stir-fry, which is spiked with
green chile.*

cook's tip

*Since most of the heat of chiles
comes from the seeds, remove them
before cooking if you want a milder
flavor. Be very careful when
handling chiles—do not touch your
face or eyes as the chile juice can
be very painful. Always wash your
hands after preparing chiles.*

Heat the oil in a preheated wok or heavy-bottomed skillet. Add the
chicken, season to taste with salt and pepper to taste, and stir-fry over
medium heat for about 4 minutes.

Add the shallots, garlic, gingerroot, and green chile and stir-fry the mixture
for an additional 2 minutes.

Add the sliced red and green bell peppers and zucchini and stir-fry for
about 1 minute.

Stir in the almonds, cinnamon, oyster sauce, and creamed coconut and
season to taste with salt and pepper. Stir-fry for 1 minute to heat through
and then serve immediately.

spanish chicken with shrimp

serves 4

5–10 minutes

1 hour 5 minutes

4 chicken quarters
1 tbsp olive oil
1 red bell pepper, seeded and sliced
1 onion, sliced
2 garlic cloves, crushed
14 oz/400 g canned chopped
    tomatoes

generous 3/4 cup dry white wine
4 tbsp chopped fresh oregano
salt and pepper
4 1/2 oz/125 g chorizo sausage
4 1/2 oz/125 g cooked, shelled shrimp
rice, to serve

This unusual dish, with its mixture of chicken and shellfish, is typically Spanish. The basis of this recipe is sofrito, a slow-cooked mixture of onion and tomato in olive oil, with garlic and bell peppers.

cook's tip

Chorizo is a spicy Spanish sausage made with pork and a hot pepper such as cayenne or pimento. It is available from large supermarkets and specialty butchers.

Remove the skin from the chicken quarters. Heat the oil in a wide, heavy-bottomed pan and fry the chicken, turning occasionally, until golden brown.

Add the bell pepper and onion to the pan and fry gently to soften.

Add the garlic with the tomatoes, wine, and oregano. Season well with salt and pepper, then bring to a boil, cover, and simmer gently for 45 minutes, or until the chicken is tender and the juices run clear when the thickest part of the chicken is pierced with a skewer.

Thinly slice the chorizo and add to the pan together with the shrimp, then simmer for an additional 5 minutes. Adjust the seasoning to taste and serve with rice.

cajun chicken gumbo

serves 2

5 minutes

about 25 minutes

1 tbsp corn oil
4 chicken thighs
1 small onion, diced
2 celery stalks, diced
1 small green bell pepper, seeded
   and diced

scant 1/2 cup long-grain rice
1 1/4 cups chicken stock
1 small fresh red chile
9 oz/250 g okra
1 tbsp tomato paste
salt and pepper

If you're cooking for one, simply halve the ingredients; the cooking time should stay the same.

Heat the oil in a wide pan and fry the chicken until golden. Remove the chicken from the pan using a perforated spoon. Stir in the onion, celery, and bell pepper and fry for 1 minute. Pour off any excess fat.

Add the rice and fry, stirring briskly, for an additional minute. Add the stock and heat until boiling.

Thinly slice the chile and trim the okra. Add to the pan with the tomato paste. Season to taste with salt and pepper.

Return the chicken to the pan and stir. Cover tightly and simmer gently for 15 minutes, or until the rice is tender and all the liquid absorbed, and the chicken is tender and the juices run clear when the thickest part is pierced with a skewer. Stir occasionally, and if the mixture becomes too dry, add a little extra stock to moisten. Serve immediately.

cook's tip

The whole chile makes the dish hot and spicy—if you prefer a milder flavor, discard the seeds.

variation

You can replace the chicken with 9 oz/250 g cooked, shelled shrimp and 3 oz/85 g belly of pork, if desired. Slice the pork and fry in the oil before adding the onions, and add the shrimp 5 minutes before the end of the cooking time.

spicy chicken tortillas

serves 4

5 minutes

30–35 minutes

2 tbsp oil

8 skinless, boneless chicken thighs, sliced

1 onion, chopped

2 garlic cloves, chopped

1 tsp cumin seeds, coarsely crushed

2 large dried chiles, sliced

14 oz/400 g canned tomatoes

14 oz/400 g canned red kidney beans, drained

^{2}/$_3$ cup chicken stock

2 tsp sugar

salt and pepper

lime wedges, to garnish

to serve

1 large ripe avocado

1 lime

8 soft tortillas

generous 1 cup thick plain yogurt

Serve these easy-to-prepare tortillas to friends or as a special family supper. The chicken filling has a mild, mellow spicy heat and a fresh salad makes a perfect accompaniment.

variation

For a vegetarian filling, replace the chicken with 14 oz/400 g canned pinto or cannellini beans and use vegetable stock instead of the chicken stock.

Heat the oil in a large skillet or wok, add the chicken, and fry for 3 minutes until golden. Add the onion and fry for 5 minutes, stirring, until browned. Add the garlic, cumin, and chiles, with their seeds, and cook for about 1 minute.

Add the tomatoes, kidney beans, stock, sugar, and salt and pepper to taste. Bring to a boil, breaking up the tomatoes. Cover and simmer for 15 minutes. Remove the lid and cook for 5 minutes, stirring occasionally, until the sauce has thickened.

Halve the avocado, discard the pit, and scoop out the flesh on to a plate. Mash the avocado with a fork. Cut half of the lime into 8 thin wedges. Squeeze the juice from the remaining lime over the avocado.

Warm the tortillas following the instructions on the package. Put 2 tortillas on each serving plate, fill with the chicken mixture, and top with spoonfuls of avocado and yogurt. Garnish the tortillas with lime wedges.

fish & seafood

The range of seafood available these days is very extensive, but sometimes it is difficult to know how to cook unfamiliar fish. The answer might be to put it into a pot and make a fabulous stew—Seafood Stew (see page 130) is incredibly easy to make and equally delicious.

This section is packed with recipes with an international flavor, including Moroccan Fish Tagine (see page 138), Thai Green Fish Curry (see page 152), and the Mexican Shellfish Chili (see page 148). There are also contemporary takes on traditional favorites, such as Modern Kedgeree (see page 142) and Seafood Lasagna (see page 154). A little sophistication is also introduced with the colorful Crab Risotto (see page 146).

The following pages include ideas for preparing every kind of seafood, from shrimp and salmon to angler fish and squid. Whether you are looking for a hot curry, a warming casserole, or a pasta or rice dish, you are bound to find a meal to suit the occasion.

celery & salt cod

casserole

serves 4

10 minutes,
plus 8 hours soaking

20–25 minutes

9 oz/250 g salt cod, soaked overnight
1 tbsp oil
4 shallots, finely chopped
2 garlic cloves, chopped
3 celery stalks, chopped
14 oz/400 g canned chopped
   tomatoes

2/3 cup fish stock
1/2 cup pine nuts
2 tbsp coarsely chopped
   fresh tarragon
2 tbsp capers
crusty bread or mashed potatoes,
   to serve

Salt cod is dried and salted in order to preserve it. It has an unusual flavor, which goes particularly well with the celery in this dish.

cook's tip

Salt cod is a useful ingredient to keep in the pantry—once soaked, it can be used in the same way as any other fish. It does, however, have a stronger flavor than normal, and it is, of course, slightly salty. It can be bought from fish dealers, larger supermarkets, and delis.

Drain the salt cod, rinse it under plenty of cold running water, and drain again thoroughly. Remove and discard any skin and bones. Pat the fish dry with paper towels and cut it into chunks.

Heat the oil in a large skillet. Add the shallots and garlic and cook for 2–3 minutes. Add the celery and cook for an additional 2 minutes, then add the tomatoes and stock.

Bring the mixture to a boil, then reduce the heat and leave to simmer for 5 minutes.

Add the fish and cook for 10 minutes, or until tender.

Meanwhile, put the pine nuts on to a cookie sheet. Put under a preheated broiler and toast for 2–3 minutes, or until golden.

Stir the tarragon, capers, and pine nuts into the fish casserole and heat gently to warm through.

Transfer to serving plates and serve at once with fresh crusty bread or mashed potatoes.

seafood stew

serves 4–6

15–20 minutes,
plus 30 minutes soaking

25–30 minutes

8 oz/225 g live clams
1 lb 9 oz/700 g mixed fish, such as
    sea bass, skate, red snapper, and
    rockfish
12–18 raw jumbo shrimp
about 3 tbsp olive oil
1 large onion, finely chopped
2 garlic cloves, very finely chopped
2 tomatoes, halved, seeded,
    and chopped

3 cups fish stock
1 tbsp tomato paste
1 tsp chopped fresh thyme
pinch of saffron strands
pinch of sugar
salt and pepper
finely chopped fresh parsley,
    to garnish

*Similar to Bouillabaisse, this
meal-in-a-pot should contain the
best of the day's catch—even if
it's from a supermarket.*

Soak the clams in a bowl of lightly salted water for 30 minutes. Rinse them under cold running water and lightly scrub to remove any sand from the shells. Discard any broken clams or open clams that do not shut when firmly tapped with the back of a knife, as these will be unsafe to eat.

Prepare the fish as necessary, removing any skin and bones, then cut into bite-size chunks.

To prepare the shrimp, break off the heads. Peel off the shells, leaving the tails intact, if wished. Using a small knife, make a slit along the back of each and remove the thin black vein. Set all the seafood aside.

Heat the oil in a large pan. Add the onion and cook for 5 minutes, stirring. Add the garlic and cook for an additional 2 minutes, or until the onion is soft but not brown.

Add the tomatoes, stock, tomato paste, thyme, saffron, and sugar, then bring to a boil, stirring to dissolve the tomato paste. Reduce the heat, cover, and simmer the stew for 15 minutes. Season to taste with salt and pepper.

Add the seafood and simmer until the clams open and the fish flakes easily. Discard any clams that do not open. Garnish with chopped parsley and serve immediately.

simmered squid

serves 4

10 minutes

25 minutes

3 tbsp extra virgin olive oil

2 lb/900 g cleaned squid, cut into rings and tentacles

salt and pepper

1 onion, chopped

3 garlic cloves, chopped

14 oz/400 g canned chopped tomatoes

1/2–1 fresh mild green chile, seeded and chopped

1 tbsp finely chopped fresh parsley

1/4 tsp chopped fresh thyme

1/4 tsp chopped fresh oregano

1/4 tsp chopped fresh marjoram

pinch of ground cinnamon

pinch of allspice

pinch of sugar

15–20 pimento-stuffed green olives, sliced

1 tbsp capers

1 tbsp chopped fresh cilantro, to garnish

This flavorsome squid dish from Vera Cruz in Mexico would be good with warmed flour tortillas, for do-it-yourself tacos.

Heat the oil in a pan and lightly fry the squid until it turns opaque. Season to taste with salt and pepper and remove the squid from the pan with a perforated spoon.

Add the onion and garlic to the remaining oil in the pan and cook until softened. Stir in the tomatoes, chile, herbs, cinnamon, allspice, sugar, and olives. Cover and cook over medium–low heat for 5–10 minutes, or until the mixture thickens slightly. Uncover the pan and cook for an additional 5 minutes to concentrate the flavors and reduce the liquid.

Stir in the reserved squid and any of the juices that have gathered. Add the capers and heat through.

Adjust the seasoning if necessary, then serve immediately, garnished with fresh cilantro.

fideua

serves 4

10 minutes

25 minutes

3 tbsp olive oil

1 large onion, chopped

2 garlic cloves, finely chopped

pinch of crumbled saffron strands

1/2 tsp paprika

3 tomatoes, peeled, seeded, and chopped

12 oz/350 g egg vermicelli, broken into 2-inch/5-cm lengths

2/3 cup white wine

1 1/4 cups fish stock

12 large raw shrimp

18 live mussels, scrubbed and bearded

12 oz/350 g cleaned squid, cut into rings

18 small live clams, scrubbed

2 tbsp chopped fresh parsley

salt and pepper

lemon wedges, to serve

Fideua is a pasta dish which can be found south of Valencia, in western Spain. It is very like a paella but is made with very fine pasta.

variation

Use whatever combination of seafood you prefer. Try lobster, shrimp, and angler fish.

Heat the oil in a large skillet or paella pan. Add the onion and cook over low heat for 5 minutes until softened. Add the garlic and cook for an additional 30 seconds. Add the saffron and paprika and stir well. Add the tomatoes and cook for an additional 2–3 minutes, or until the tomatoes have collapsed.

Add the vermicelli and stir well. Add the wine and boil rapidly until it has been absorbed.

Add the stock, shrimp, mussels, squid, and clams. Stir and return to low simmer for 10 minutes until the shrimp and squid are cooked through and the mussels and clams have opened. Discard any that remain shut. The stock should be almost completely absorbed.

Add the parsley and season to taste with salt and pepper. Serve immediately in warmed bowls with lemon wedges.

cotriade

serves 4

2 minutes, plus
10 minutes infusing

about 45 minutes

large pinch of saffron strands
2½ cups hot fish stock
1 tbsp olive oil
2 tbsp butter
1 onion, sliced
2 garlic cloves, chopped
1 leek, sliced
1 small fennel bulb, thinly sliced
1 lb/450 g potatoes, cut into chunks
⅔ cup dry white wine

1 tbsp chopped fresh thyme
2 bay leaves
4 ripe tomatoes, peeled and chopped
2 lb/900 g mixed fish fillets, such as
    haddock, hake, mackerel, and red
    or gray mullet, coarsely chopped
2 tbsp chopped fresh parsley
salt and pepper
crusty bread, to serve

*This is a rich French stew of
fish and vegetables, flavored
with saffron and herbs. The fish
and vegetables, and the soup,
are served separately.*

variation

*Once the fish and vegetables have
been cooked, you could process the
soup in a food processor or blender
and pass it through a strainer to
give a smooth fish soup.*

Using a mortar and pestle, crumble the saffron and add it to the stock. Stir
the mixture and set aside to infuse for at least 10 minutes.

Heat the oil and butter together in a large, heavy-bottomed pan. Add the
onion and cook over low heat, stirring occasionally, for 4–5 minutes, or
until softened. Add the garlic, leek, fennel, and potatoes. Cover and cook
for an additional 10–15 minutes, or until the vegetables are softened.

Add the wine and simmer rapidly for 3–4 minutes, or until reduced by
about half. Add the thyme, bay leaves, and tomatoes and stir well. Add the
saffron-infused stock. Bring to a boil, cover, and simmer over low heat for
15 minutes, or until all the vegetables are tender.

Add the fish, return to a boil, and simmer for an additional 3–4 minutes, or
until all the fish is tender. Add the parsley and season to taste with salt and
pepper. Using a perforated spoon, transfer the fish and vegetables to a
warmed serving dish. Serve the soup with plenty of crusty bread.

moroccan fish tagine

serves 4

5 minutes

about 1 hour 10 minutes

2 tbsp olive oil
1 large onion, finely chopped
pinch of saffron strands
1/2 tsp ground cinnamon
1 tsp ground coriander
1/2 tsp ground cumin
1/2 tsp turmeric
7 oz/200 g canned chopped tomatoes

1 1/4 cups fish stock
4 small red mullet, cleaned, boned,
    and heads and tails removed
1/3 cup pitted green olives
1 tbsp chopped preserved lemon
3 tbsp chopped fresh cilantro
salt and pepper
couscous, to serve

A tagine is a Moroccan cooking vessel consisting of an earthenware dish with a domed lid that has a steam hole in the top.

cook's tip

For preserved lemons, take enough lemons to fill a preserving jar. Quarter them lengthwise without cutting all the way through. Pack them with 2 oz/55 g sea salt per lemon. Add the juice of 1 more lemon and top up with water to cover. Leave for 1 month.

Heat the oil in a large pan or flameproof casserole. Add the onion and cook gently, stirring occasionally, for 10 minutes, without coloring, until softened. Add the saffron, cinnamon, coriander, cumin, and turmeric and cook for an additional 30 seconds, stirring.

Add the chopped tomatoes and stock and stir well. Bring to a boil, cover, and simmer for 15 minutes. Uncover and simmer for an additional 20–35 minutes, or until thickened.

Cut each red mullet in half, then add the pieces to the pan, pushing them into the sauce. Simmer the tagine gently for an additional 5–6 minutes, or until the fish is just cooked.

Carefully stir in the olives, preserved lemon, and the chopped cilantro. Season to taste with salt and pepper and serve with couscous.

spanish fish stew

serves 4

15–20 minutes

about 55 minutes

5 tbsp olive oil

2 large onions, finely chopped

2 tomatoes, peeled, seeded, and diced

2 slices white bread, crusts removed

4 almonds, toasted

3 garlic cloves, roughly chopped

12 oz/350 g cooked lobster

7 oz/200 g cleaned squid

7 oz/200 g angler fish fillet

7 oz/200 g cod fillet, skinned

salt and pepper

1 tbsp all-purpose flour

6 large raw shrimp

6 jumbo shrimp

18 live mussels, scrubbed and bearded

8 small live clams, scrubbed

1 tbsp chopped fresh parsley

1/2 cup brandy

This is an impressive-looking Catalan dish using two classic Spanish cooking methods—the sofrito *and the* picada.

Heat 3 tablespoons of the oil and cook the onions over low heat for 10–15 minutes, or until golden. Add the tomatoes and cook until they have collapsed.

Heat 1 tablespoon of the remaining oil and fry the slices of bread until crisp. Break into pieces and put into a mortar with the almonds and 2 garlic cloves. Pound to a fine paste. Alternatively, process in a food processor.

Split the lobster lengthwise. Remove and discard the intestinal vein, the stomach sac, and the spongy gills. Crack the claws and remove the meat. Take out the flesh from the tail and chop into large chunks. Slice the squid into rings. Cut the angler fish and cod into chunks.

Season the angler fish, cod, and lobster to taste with salt and pepper and dust with flour. Heat a little of the remaining oil and separately brown the angler fish, cod, lobster, squid, and shrimp. Arrange the seafood in a flame-proof casserole as the pieces brown.

Add the mussels and clams and the remaining garlic and parsley. Set the pan over low heat. Pour over the brandy and ignite. When the flames have died down, add the tomato mixture and just enough water to cover. Bring to a boil, then reduce the heat and simmer for 3–4 minutes, or until the mussels and clams have opened. Stir in the bread mixture and season to taste with salt and pepper. Simmer for an additional 5 minutes and serve.

modern kedgeree

serves 4

10 minutes

about 35 minutes

2 tbsp butter
1 tbsp olive oil
1 onion, finely chopped
1 garlic clove, finely chopped
generous ¾ cup long-grain rice
1¾ cups fish stock
6 oz/175 g salmon fillet, skinned
    and chopped

3 oz/85 g smoked salmon, chopped
2 tbsp heavy cream
2 tbsp chopped fresh dill
3 scallions, finely chopped
salt and pepper
fresh dill sprigs and lemon slices,
    to garnish

This is a modern version of the classic dish, using smoked salmon as well as fresh salmon and lots of fresh herbs—perfect for a dinner party.

cook's tip

Use smoked salmon trimmings for a budget dish.

Melt the butter with the oil in a large pan. Add the onion and cook over low heat for 10 minutes, or until softened but not colored. Add the garlic and cook for an additional 30 seconds.

Add the rice and cook, stirring constantly, for 2–3 minutes, or until transparent. Add the stock and stir well. Bring to a boil, cover, and simmer very gently for 10 minutes.

Add the salmon fillet and the smoked salmon and stir well, adding a little more stock or water if the mixture seems dry. Cook for an additional 6–8 minutes, or until the fish and rice are tender and all the stock is absorbed.

Turn off the heat and stir in the cream, chopped dill, and scallions. Season to taste with salt and pepper and serve immediately, garnished with dill sprigs and lemon slices.

shrimp & asparagus
risotto

serves 4

10 minutes

about 45 minutes

1 quart vegetable stock
13 oz/375 g asparagus, cut into
  2-inch/5-cm lengths
2 tbsp olive oil
1 onion, finely chopped
1 garlic clove, finely chopped
1¾ cups risotto rice

1 lb/450 g raw jumbo shrimp, peeled
  and deveined
2 tbsp tapenade (olive paste)
2 tbsp chopped fresh basil
salt and pepper
Parmesan cheese shavings, to garnish

An unusual and striking dish with fresh shrimp and asparagus is very simple to prepare and ideal for impromptu supper parties.

Bring the stock to a boil in a large pan. Add the asparagus and cook for 3 minutes until just tender. Strain, reserving the stock, and refresh the asparagus under cold running water. Drain and set aside.

Heat the oil in a large, heavy-bottomed skillet. Add the onion and cook over low heat, stirring occasionally, for 5 minutes until softened. Add the garlic and cook for an additional 30 seconds. Add the rice and cook, stirring constantly, for 1–2 minutes, or until the rice is coated with the oil and slightly translucent.

Keep the stock over low heat. Increase the heat under the skillet to medium and begin adding the stock, a ladleful at a time, stirring well between additions. Continue until almost all the stock has been absorbed. This should take 20–25 minutes.

Add the shrimp and asparagus with the last ladleful of stock and cook for an additional 5 minutes until the shrimp and rice are tender and the stock has been absorbed. Remove from the heat.

Stir in the tapenade, basil, and salt and pepper to taste and set aside for 1 minute. Serve immediately, garnished with Parmesan shavings.

crab risotto

serves 4–6

10–15 minutes

about 40 minutes

2–3 large red bell peppers, seeded and halved

3 tbsp olive oil

1 onion, finely chopped

1 small fennel bulb, finely chopped

2 celery stalks, finely chopped

$1/4$–$1/2$ tsp cayenne pepper

$1^2/3$ cups risotto rice

1 lb 12 oz/800 g canned chopped tomatoes, drained

4 tbsp dry white vermouth (optional)

$1^1/4$ quarts fish or chicken stock, simmering

1 lb/450 g fresh cooked crabmeat

4 tbsp lemon juice

2–4 tbsp chopped fresh parsley or chervil

salt and pepper

seasonal salad, to serve

A different way to make the most of crab, this rich-tasting and colorful risotto is full of interesting flavors.

Broil the bell peppers until the skins are charred. Transfer to a plastic bag and twist to seal. When cool enough to handle, peel off the charred skins, working over a bowl to catch the juices. Chop the flesh and set aside, reserving the juices.

Heat the oil in a large, heavy-bottomed skillet. Add the onion, fennel, and celery and cook over low heat, stirring occasionally, for 2–3 minutes, or until the vegetables are softened. Add the cayenne pepper and rice and cook, stirring frequently, for 2 minutes, or until the rice is translucent and well coated.

Stir in the chopped tomatoes and vermouth, if using. The liquid will bubble and steam rapidly. When the liquid is almost absorbed, add a ladleful (about 1 cup) of the simmering stock. Cook, stirring constantly, until the liquid is completely absorbed.

Continue adding the stock, about half a ladleful at a time, allowing each addition to be absorbed before adding the next. This should take 20–25 minutes. The risotto should have a creamy consistency and the rice should be tender but still firm to the bite.

Stir in the red bell peppers and reserved juices, the crabmeat, lemon juice, and parsley or chervil and heat through. Season to taste with salt and pepper. Serve the risotto immediately, with a side salad.

shellfish chili

serves 4

5 minutes, plus
1 hour marinating

45 minutes

4 oz/115 g raw shrimp, shelled and
deveined

9 oz/250 g raw prepared scallops,
thawed if frozen

4 oz/115 g angler fish fillet,
cut into chunks

1 lime, peeled and thinly sliced

1 tbsp chili powder

1 tsp ground cumin

3 tbsp chopped fresh cilantro

2 garlic cloves, finely chopped

1 fresh green chile, seeded and
chopped

3 tbsp corn oil

1 onion, roughly chopped

1 red bell pepper, seeded and
roughly chopped

1 yellow bell pepper, seeded and
roughly chopped

1/4 tsp ground cloves

pinch of ground cinnamon

pinch of cayenne pepper

salt

1 1/2 cups fish stock

14 oz/400 g canned chopped
tomatoes

14 oz/400 g canned red kidney beans,
drained and rinsed

*For an authentic Mexican treat,
serve this seafood extravaganza
with ready-made tortillas, heated
through in a dry skillet.*

Put the shrimp, scallops, angler fish chunks, and lime slices into a large, nonmetallic dish with 1/4 teaspoon of the chili powder, 1/4 teaspoon of the
ground cumin, 1 tablespoon of the chopped cilantro, half the garlic, the
green chile, and 1 tablespoon of the oil. Cover with plastic wrap and let
stand to marinate for up to 1 hour.

Meanwhile, heat 1 tablespoon of the remaining oil in a flameproof
casserole or large, heavy-bottomed pan. Add the onion, the remaining
garlic, and the red and yellow bell peppers and cook over low heat, stirring
occasionally, for 5 minutes, or until softened. Add the remaining chili
powder, the remaining cumin, the cloves, cinnamon, and cayenne pepper
with the remaining oil, if necessary, and season to taste with salt. Cook,
stirring, for 5 minutes, then gradually stir in the stock and the tomatoes and
their juice. Partially cover the casserole and simmer for 25 minutes.

Add the beans to the tomato mixture and spoon the fish and shellfish on
top. Cover and cook for 10 minutes, or until the fish and shellfish are
cooked through. Sprinkle with the remaining cilantro and serve.

goan fish curry

serves 4

5–10 minutes, plus
20 minutes standing

about 15 minutes

1 lb 10 oz/750 g angler fish fillet, cut
  into chunks
1 tbsp cider vinegar
1 tsp salt
1 tsp ground turmeric
3 tbsp vegetable oil
2 garlic cloves, crushed
1 small onion, finely chopped
2 tsp ground coriander

1 tsp cayenne pepper
2 tsp paprika
2 tbsp tamarind pulp plus 2 tbsp
  boiling water (see method)
3 oz/85 g creamed coconut, cut
  into pieces
1 1/4 cups warm water
plain boiled rice, to serve

*Goan cuisine is famous for seafood
and vindaloo dishes, which tend to
be very hot. This recipe is a mild
curry, but very flavorsome.*

Put the fish on a plate and drizzle the vinegar over it. Combine half the salt and half the turmeric and sprinkle evenly over the fish. Cover and set aside for 20 minutes.

Heat the oil in a heavy-bottomed skillet and add the garlic. Brown slightly, then add the onion and cook, stirring occasionally, for 3–4 minutes, or until soft but not browned. Add the coriander and stir for 1 minute.

Mix the remaining turmeric and salt, cayenne pepper, and paprika with about 2 tablespoons water to make a paste. Add to the skillet and cook over low heat for 1–2 minutes.

Stir the tamarind pulp and boiling water together in a small bowl. When thickened and the pulp has come away from the seeds, rub through a strainer. Discard the seeds.

Add the coconut, warm water, and tamarind paste to the pan and stir until the coconut has dissolved. Add the fish and any juices on the plate and simmer gently for 4–5 minutes, or until the sauce has thickened and the fish is just tender. Serve on a bed of plain boiled rice.

thai green fish curry

serves 4

5–10 minutes

about 20 minutes

2 tbsp vegetable oil

I garlic clove, chopped

I small eggplant, diced

½ cup coconut cream

2 tbsp Thai fish sauce

I tsp sugar

8 oz/225 g firm white fish, such as cod, haddock, and halibut, cut into pieces

½ cup fish stock

2 kaffir lime leaves, finely shredded

about 15 fresh Thai basil leaves, if available, or ordinary fresh basil

plain boiled rice or noodles, to serve

green curry paste

5 fresh green chiles, seeded and chopped

2 tsp chopped lemon grass

I large shallot, chopped

2 garlic cloves, chopped

I tsp grated fresh gingerroot or galangal

¼ bunch fresh cilantro, chopped

½ tsp ground coriander

¼ tsp ground cumin

I kaffir lime leaf, finely chopped

I tsp shrimp paste (optional)

½ tsp salt

This pale green curry paste can be used as the basis for all sorts of Thai dishes. It is also delicious with chicken and beef.

Make the curry paste. Put all the ingredients into a blender or spice grinder and blend to a smooth paste, adding a little water if necessary. Alternatively, pound together all the ingredients, using a mortar and pestle, until smooth. Set aside.

Heat the oil in a skillet or wok until almost smoking. Add the garlic and fry until golden. Add the curry paste and stir-fry for a few seconds before adding the eggplant. Stir-fry for 4–5 minutes, or until softened.

Add the coconut cream. Bring to a boil and stir until the cream thickens and curdles slightly. Add the fish sauce and sugar and stir into the mixture.

Add the fish and stock. Simmer, stirring occasionally, for 3–4 minutes, or until the fish is just tender. Add the lime leaves and basil, and then cook for an additional minute.

Transfer the curry to a warmed serving dish and serve with plain boiled rice or noodles.

seafood lasagna

serves 6

5 minutes, plus
10 minutes standing

about 1 hour 10 minutes

4 tbsp butter, plus extra for greasing

6 tbsp all-purpose flour

1 tsp mustard powder

2½ cups milk

2 tbsp olive oil

1 onion, chopped

2 garlic cloves, finely chopped

1 tbsp chopped fresh thyme

1 lb/450 g mixed mushrooms, sliced

⅔ cup white wine

14 oz/400 g canned chopped
  tomatoes

salt and pepper

1 lb/450 g mixed skinless white fish
  fillets, cubed

8 oz/225 g raw prepared scallops

4–6 sheets fresh lasagne

8 oz/225 g mozzarella cheese,
  chopped

*A rich dish of pasta layers,
with seafood and mushrooms
in a tomato sauce, topped
with béchamel sauce and
baked until golden.*

Preheat the oven to 400°F/200°C. Melt the butter in a pan. Add the flour and mustard powder and stir until smooth. Simmer gently for 2 minutes without coloring. Gradually add the milk, whisking until smooth. Bring to a boil, then reduce the heat and simmer for 2 minutes. Remove from the heat and set aside. Cover the surface of the sauce with plastic wrap to prevent a skin from forming.

Heat the oil in a skillet and add the onion, garlic, and thyme. Cook gently for 5 minutes until softened. Add the mushrooms and fry for an additional 5 minutes until softened. Stir in the wine and boil rapidly until nearly evaporated. Stir in the tomatoes. Bring to a boil, then reduce the heat and simmer, covered, for 15 minutes. Season to taste with salt and pepper and set aside.

Grease a lasagna dish. Spoon half the tomato sauce in the dish and top with half the fish and scallops.

Layer half the lasagna over the fish, pour over half the white sauce, and add half the cubes of mozzarella. Repeat these layers, finishing with the white sauce and mozzarella.

Bake the lasagna in the preheated oven for 35–40 minutes, or until bubbling and golden and the fish is cooked through. Remove from the oven and let stand on a heat-resistant surface or mat for 10 minutes before serving.

vegetables

Nutritionists tell us that we should eat more vegetables, but it isn't always easy to persuade the family to eat up their greens. This chapter provides the answer, with a spectacular collection of mouthwatering vegetable dishes, from Roasted Pumpkin Risotto (see page 208) to a delicious and unusual Winter Vegetable Cobbler (see page 170).

Beans, lentils, bell peppers, zucchini, eggplant, broccoli, cauliflower, onions, tomatoes, and even the humble potato take a starring role, and are combined with each other for a colorful, melt-in-the-mouth medley which will satisfy even the hungriest appetite. If you are in the mood for something hot, try Vegetable Chili (see page 200), Mixed Vegetable Balti (see page 196), or Red Curry with Cashews (see page 192). If you are looking for something a little more comforting, Red Bean Stew & Dumplings (see page 182) or Potato & Mushroom Hash (see page 168) will fit the bill perfectly.

A vegetarian entrée is an easy way to ring the changes in the weekly menu, and nut-, bean-, or lentil-based dishes can be just as nutritious as a meat or fish dish. Whatever your favorite vegetable, there will be something in this section to tempt you.

winter vegetable casserole

serves 4

10 minutes

40 minutes

1 tbsp olive oil	6 tbsp dry white wine
1 red onion, halved and sliced	14 oz/400 g canned chickpeas, drained
3 garlic cloves, crushed	
8 oz/225 g spinach	1 bay leaf
1 fennel bulb, cut into 8 wedges	1 tsp ground coriander
1 red bell pepper, seeded and diced	1/2 tsp paprika
1 tbsp all-purpose flour	salt and pepper
2 cups vegetable stock	fennel fronds, to garnish

This hearty supper dish is best served with plenty of warm crusty bread to mop up the delicious juices.

variation

Use other canned peas or mixed beans instead of the chickpeas, if you prefer.

Heat the oil in a large, flameproof casserole. Add the onion and garlic and cook over low heat, stirring frequently, for 1 minute. Add the spinach and cook, stirring occasionally, for 4 minutes, or until wilted.

Add the fennel and red bell pepper and cook, stirring, for 2 minutes.

Stir in the flour and cook, stirring constantly, for 1 minute.

Add the stock, wine, chickpeas, bay leaf, ground coriander, and paprika, cover, and simmer for 30 minutes. Season to taste with salt and pepper, garnish with fennel fronds, and serve immediately, straight from the casserole.

spicy potato casserole

serves 4

15 minutes

about 35 minutes

generous ⅓ cup olive oil

2 red onions, cut into 8 wedges

3 garlic cloves, crushed

2 tsp ground cumin

2 tsp ground coriander

pinch of cayenne pepper

1 carrot, thickly sliced

2 small turnips, quartered

1 zucchini, sliced

1 lb 2 oz/500 g potatoes, thickly sliced

grated rind and juice of 2 large lemons

1¼ cups vegetable stock

salt and pepper

2 tbsp chopped fresh cilantro

This is based on a Moroccan dish in which potatoes are spiced with coriander and cumin and cooked in a lemon sauce.

cook's tip

Check the vegetables while they are cooking, because they may begin to stick to the casserole. Add a little more boiling water or stock if necessary.

Heat the oil in a flameproof casserole. Add the onion and sauté over medium heat, stirring frequently, for 3 minutes.

Add the garlic and cook for 30 seconds. Stir in the cumin, coriander, and cayenne pepper and cook, stirring constantly, for 1 minute.

Add the carrot, turnips, zucchini, and potatoes and stir to coat in the oil.

Add the lemon rind and juice and the stock. Season to taste with salt and pepper. Cover and cook over medium heat, stirring occasionally, for 20–30 minutes, or until tender.

Remove the lid, sprinkle in the chopped fresh cilantro, and stir well. Serve immediately.

vegetable hotchpotch

serves 4

25 minutes

about 55 minutes

1 lb 5 oz/600 g potatoes, thinly sliced
2 tbsp vegetable oil
1 red onion, halved and sliced
1 leek, sliced
2 garlic cloves, crushed
1 carrot, cut into chunks
3½ oz/100 g broccoli florets
3½ oz/100 g cauliflower florets
2 small turnips, quartered

1 tbsp all-purpose flour
3 cups vegetable stock
⅔ cup dry hard cider
1 apple, cored and sliced
2 tbsp chopped fresh sage
pinch of cayenne pepper
salt and pepper
1¾ oz/50 g Cheddar cheese, grated

In this recipe, mixed vegetables are cooked under a layer of potatoes, topped with cheese and cooked until golden brown.

Preheat the oven to 375°F/190°C. Cook the potato slices in a pan of boiling water for 10 minutes. Drain thoroughly and reserve.

Heat the oil in a flameproof casserole. Add the onion, leek, and garlic to the oil and sauté, stirring occasionally, for 2–3 minutes.

Add the remaining vegetables and cook, stirring constantly, for an additional 3–4 minutes.

Stir in the flour and cook for 1 minute. Gradually add the stock and hard cider and bring to a boil. Add the apple, sage, and cayenne pepper and season to taste with salt and pepper.

Remove from the heat and transfer the vegetables to an ovenproof dish.

Arrange the potato slices on top of the vegetable mixture to cover.

Sprinkle the grated cheese on top of the potato slices and cook in the preheated oven for 30–35 minutes, or until the potato is golden brown and beginning to crisp around the edges. Serve immediately, straight from the dish.

lentil & rice casserole

serves 4

15 minutes

about 35 minutes

generous 1 cup red lentils
generous ¼ cup long-grain rice
1 quart vegetable stock
1 leek, cut into chunks
3 garlic cloves, crushed
14 oz/400 g canned chopped
  tomatoes
1 tsp ground cumin
1 tsp chili powder

1 tsp garam masala
1 red bell pepper, seeded and sliced
3½ oz/100 g small broccoli florets
8 baby corn cobs, halved lengthwise
2 oz/55 g green beans, halved
1 tbsp shredded fresh basil
salt and pepper
fresh basil sprigs, to garnish

*This is a really hearty dish,
perfect for cold days when a
filling hot dish is just what you
need to keep the winter out.*

variation

*You can vary the rice in
this recipe—use brown or
wild rice, if you prefer.*

Put the lentils, rice, and stock into a large, flameproof casserole and cook over low heat, stirring occasionally, for 20 minutes.

Add the leek, garlic, tomatoes and their juice, cumin, chili powder, garam masala, sliced bell pepper, broccoli, corn cobs, and green beans to the casserole.

Bring the mixture to a boil, then reduce the heat, cover, and simmer for an additional 10–15 minutes, or until the vegetables are tender.

Add the shredded basil and season to taste with salt and pepper.

Garnish with fresh basil sprigs and serve immediately.

potato hash

serves 4

5 minutes

about 30 minutes

2 tbsp butter
1 red onion, halved and sliced
1 carrot, diced
1 oz/25 g green beans, halved
2 lb/900 g waxy potatoes, diced
2 tbsp all-purpose flour

2½ cups vegetable stock
8 oz/225 g firm tofu (bean curd), diced
salt and pepper
chopped fresh parsley, to garnish

This is a variation of the traditional beef hash, which was originally made with salt beef and leftovers, and served to seafaring New Englanders.

Melt the butter in a large, heavy-bottomed skillet. Add the onion, carrot, green beans, and potatoes and fry over fairly low heat, stirring constantly, for 5–7 minutes, or until the vegetables begin to turn golden brown.

Add the flour to the pan and cook, stirring constantly, for 1 minute. Gradually pour in the stock, stirring constantly.

Reduce the heat to low and simmer for 15 minutes, or until the potatoes are tender.

Add the diced tofu (bean curd) to the pan and cook for an additional 5 minutes. Season to taste with salt and pepper.

Sprinkle the chopped fresh parsley over the top of the hash to garnish and then serve it hot, straight from the skillet.

potato & mushroom hash

serves 4

5 minutes

about 30 minutes

1 ½ lb/675 g potatoes, diced
1 tbsp olive oil
2 garlic cloves, crushed
1 green bell pepper, seeded and diced
1 yellow bell pepper, seeded and diced
3 tomatoes, diced

3 oz/75 g white mushrooms, halved
1 tbsp Worcestershire sauce
2 tbsp chopped fresh basil
salt and pepper
fresh basil sprigs, to garnish
warm crusty bread, to serve

This is an easy dish which is ideal for a quick snack, packed with color and flavor. You can add any other vegetable you have at hand.

cook's tip

Most brands of Worcestershire sauce contain anchovies. When cooking for vegetarians, make sure you choose a vegetarian variety.

Cook the potatoes in a pan of boiling salted water for 7–8 minutes. Drain well and reserve.

Heat the oil in a large, heavy-bottomed skillet and cook the potatoes, stirring, for 8–10 minutes, or until browned.

Add the garlic and bell peppers to the pan and cook for 2–3 minutes.

Stir the tomatoes and mushrooms into the mixture and continue to cook, stirring, for an additional 5–6 minutes.

Stir in the Worcestershire sauce and basil and season to taste with salt and pepper.

Transfer the hash to a warmed serving dish, garnish with the fresh basil, and serve at once with crusty bread.

winter vegetable cobbler

serves 4

5–10 minutes

about 45 minutes

1 tbsp olive oil
1 garlic clove, crushed
8 small onions, halved
2 celery stalks, sliced
8 oz/225 g rutabaga, chopped
2 carrots, sliced
1/2 small cauliflower, broken into florets
8 oz/225 g mushrooms, sliced
14 oz/400 g canned chopped tomatoes
generous 1/4 cup red lentils
2 tbsp cornstarch
3–4 tbsp water

1 1/4 cups vegetable stock
2 tsp Tabasco sauce
2 tsp chopped fresh oregano
fresh oregano sprigs, to garnish

cobbler topping

generous 1 1/2 cups self-rising flour
pinch of salt
4 tbsp butter
1 cup grated sharp Cheddar cheese
2 tsp chopped fresh oregano
1 egg, lightly beaten
2/3 cup milk

Seasonal fresh vegetables are casseroled with lentils, then topped with a ring of fresh cheese biscuit rounds to make this tasty cobbler.

Preheat the oven to 350°F/180°C. Heat the oil in a skillet and cook the garlic and onions for 5 minutes. Add the celery, rutabaga, carrots, and cauliflower and cook for 2–3 minutes. Add the mushrooms, tomatoes, and lentils. Mix the cornstarch and water and stir into the pan with the stock, Tabasco, and oregano.

Transfer the vegetable mixture to an ovenproof dish, cover, and cook in the preheated oven for 20 minutes.

For the topping, sift the flour with the salt into a bowl. Rub in the butter, then stir in most of the cheese and the herbs. Beat the egg with the milk. Add enough to the dry ingredients to make a soft dough. Knead lightly, roll out the dough to 1/2 inch/1 cm thick, and cut into 2-inch/5-cm rounds.

Remove the dish from the oven and increase the temperature to 400°F/200°C. Arrange the biscuit rounds around the edge of the dish, brush with the remaining egg and milk, and sprinkle with the reserved cheese. Cook for an additional 10–12 minutes. Garnish with oregano sprigs and serve.

cheese & potato
layer bake

serves 4

5 minutes

1 hour 25 minutes

500 g/1 lb 2 oz potatoes
1 leek, sliced
3 garlic cloves, crushed
1³⁄4 oz/50 g Cheddar cheese, grated
1³⁄4 oz/50 g mozzarella cheese, grated
1 oz/25 g Parmesan cheese,
   freshly grated

2 tbsp chopped fresh flatleaf parsley,
   plus extra to garnish
salt and pepper
²⁄3 cup light cream
²⁄3 cup milk

*This really is a great side dish,
perfect for serving alongside main
meals cooked in the oven.*

cook's tip

*Potatoes make a very good basis
for a vegetable accompaniment.
They are a good source of complex
carbohydrate and contain a number
of vitamins. From the point of view
of flavor, they combine well with a
vast range of other ingredients.*

Preheat the oven to 325°F/160°C. Cook the potatoes in a pan of boiling salted water for 10 minutes. Drain well.

Cut the potatoes into thin slices. Arrange a layer of potatoes in the bottom of an ovenproof dish. Layer with a little of the sliced leek, crushed garlic, cheeses, and chopped parsley. Season to taste with salt and pepper.

Repeat the layers until all of the ingredients have been used, finishing with a layer of cheese.

Mix the cream and milk together, season to taste with salt and pepper, and pour over the potato layers.

Cook the bake in the preheated oven for 1–1¼ hours, or until the cheese topping is golden brown and bubbling and the potatoes are cooked through and tender.

Garnish the bake with chopped parsley and serve immediately.

vegetable lasagna

serves 4

5 minutes, plus
20 minutes standing

about 50 minutes

1 eggplant, sliced

salt

3 tbsp olive oil

2 garlic cloves, crushed

1 red onion, halved and sliced

3 mixed bell peppers, seeded and
    diced

8 oz/225 g mixed mushrooms, sliced

2 celery stalks, sliced

1 zucchini, diced

1/2 tsp chili powder

1/2 tsp ground cumin

2 tomatoes, chopped

1 1/4 cups strained tomatoes

2 tbsp chopped fresh basil

salt and pepper

8 pre-cooked lasagna verde sheets

cheese sauce

2 tbsp butter or margarine

1 tbsp all-purpose flour

2/3 cup vegetable stock

1 1/4 cups milk

2 3/4 oz/75 g Cheddar cheese, grated

1 tsp Dijon mustard

1 tbsp chopped fresh basil

1 egg, beaten

*This colorful and tasty lasagna
has layers of vegetables in tomato
sauce and eggplant, all topped with
a rich cheese sauce.*

Preheat the oven to 350°F/180°C. Put the eggplant slices into a colander,
sprinkle them with salt, and leave for 20 minutes. Rinse under cold running
water, drain, and reserve.

Heat the oil in a skillet and sauté the garlic and onion for 1–2 minutes. Add
the bell peppers, mushrooms, celery, and zucchini and cook, stirring
constantly, for 3–4 minutes.

Stir in the spices and cook for 1 minute. Mix in the chopped tomatoes,
strained tomatoes, and basil and season to taste with salt and pepper.

For the sauce, melt the butter or margarine in a pan, stir in the flour, and
cook for 1 minute. Remove from the heat and stir in the stock and milk.
Return to the heat and boil, stirring, for 3 minutes, or until thickened. Stir in
half the cheese, mustard, and basil. Remove from the heat, let cool slightly,
and stir in the egg.

Put half the lasagna sheets into an ovenproof dish. Top with half the
vegetable mixture, then half the eggplant. Repeat the layers and spoon the
cheese sauce on top.

Sprinkle the lasagna with the remaining cheese and cook in the preheated
oven for 40 minutes, or until the top is golden brown.

bread & butter savory

serves 4

5–10 minutes,
plus 20 minutes soaking

about 45 minutes

generous ¼ cup butter or margarine

1 bunch scallions, sliced

6 slices white or brown bread,
  crusts removed

6 oz/175 g sharp Cheddar cheese,
  grated

2 eggs

generous 1¾ cups milk

salt and pepper

fresh flatleaf parsley sprigs,
  to garnish

*Quick, simple, nutritious,
and a pleasure to eat—what more
could you ask for in an inexpensive
midweek meal?*

variation

*You can vary the vegetables
used in this dish, depending
on what you have to hand.
Shallots, mushrooms, or
tomatoes are all suitable.*

Preheat the oven to 375°F/190°C. Lightly grease a 1¼-quart ovenproof dish with a little of the butter or margarine.

Melt the remaining butter or margarine in a small pan. Add the scallions and fry over medium heat, stirring occasionally, until softened and golden.

Meanwhile, cut the bread into triangles and put half of them in the bottom of the dish. Cover with the sliced scallions and top with half the grated cheese.

Beat the eggs and milk together and season to taste with salt and pepper. Layer the remaining triangles of bread in the dish and carefully pour over the milk mixture. Let soak for 15–20 minutes.

Sprinkle the remaining cheese over the soaked bread. Cook in the preheated oven for 35–40 minutes, or until puffed up and golden brown. Garnish with parsley sprigs and serve immediately.

potato & mushroom
bake

serves 4

5 minutes

55 minutes

2 tbsp butter

1 lb 2 oz/500 g waxy potatoes, thinly sliced

5½ oz/150 g mixed mushrooms, sliced

1 tbsp chopped fresh rosemary

4 tbsp snipped fresh chives, plus extra to garnish

2 garlic cloves, crushed

⅔ cup heavy cream

salt and pepper

Use any mixture of mushrooms for this creamy layered bake. It can be served straight from the dish in which it is cooked.

cook's tip

For a special occasion, the bake may be made in a lined cake pan and then turned out to serve.

Preheat the oven to 375°F/190°C. Grease a shallow ovenproof dish with the butter.

Parboil the potatoes in a pan of boiling water for 10 minutes. Drain well. Layer a quarter of the potatoes in the bottom of the dish.

Arrange about a quarter of the mushrooms in a layer on top of the potatoes and sprinkle with a quarter each of the rosemary, snipped chives, and garlic. Continue making layers in the same order, finishing with a layer of potatoes on top.

Pour the cream over the top of the potatoes. Season to taste with salt and pepper.

Cook in the preheated oven for 45 minutes, or until the bake is golden brown and piping hot.

Garnish with snipped chives and serve immediately, straight from the dish.

pasta & bean casserole

serves 4

10 minutes,
plus 8 hours soaking

about 3 hours 30 minutes

generous 1 cup dried Great
　　Northern beans, soaked overnight
　　and drained
8 oz/225 g dried penne or other
　　short pasta shapes
salt and pepper
6 tbsp olive oil
3 ½ cups vegetable stock
2 large onions, sliced
2 garlic cloves, chopped
2 bay leaves
1 tsp dried oregano
1 tsp dried thyme

5 tbsp red wine
2 tbsp tomato paste
2 celery stalks, sliced
1 fennel bulb, sliced
4 oz/115 g mushrooms, sliced
8 oz/225 g tomatoes, sliced
1 tsp brown sugar
½ cup dry white bread crumbs

to serve
salad greens
crusty bread

*A satisfying winter dish, this
is a slow-cooked, filling meal.
The Great Northern beans
need to be soaked overnight,
so prepare well in advance.*

Preheat the oven to 350°F/180°C. Put the beans into a large pan, add water to cover, and bring to a boil. Boil the beans rapidly for 20 minutes, then drain them and set aside.

Cook the pasta for only 3 minutes in a large pan of boiling salted water, adding 1 tablespoon of the oil. Drain in a colander and set aside.

Put the beans into a large, flameproof casserole, pour in the stock, and stir in the remaining oil, the onions, garlic, bay leaves, herbs, wine, and tomato paste.

Bring to a boil, cover, and cook in the preheated oven for 2 hours.

Remove the casserole from the oven, add the reserved pasta, the sliced celery, fennel, mushrooms, and tomatoes and season to taste with salt and pepper.

Stir in the sugar and sprinkle the bread crumbs on top. Re-cover the casserole, return to the oven, and continue cooking for 1 hour. Serve straight from the casserole with salad greens and crusty bread.

red bean stew
& dumplings

serves 4

10 minutes

about 35 minutes

1 tbsp vegetable oil
1 red onion, sliced
2 celery stalks, chopped
3 1/2 cups vegetable stock
8 oz/225 g carrots, diced
8 oz/225 g potatoes, diced
8 oz/225 g zucchini, diced
4 tomatoes, peeled and chopped
2/3 cup red lentils
14 oz/400 g canned kidney beans,
    drained and rinsed
1 tsp paprika
salt and pepper

dumplings

scant 1 cup all-purpose flour
1/2 tsp salt
2 tsp baking powder
1 tsp paprika
1 tsp dried mixed herbs
1/4 cup shredded or vegetarian suet
7 tbsp water
fresh flatleaf parsley sprigs,
    to garnish

There's nothing better on a cold day than a hearty dish topped with dumplings. This recipe is very quick and easy to prepare.

Heat the oil in a flameproof casserole or a large pan. Add the onion and celery and fry over low heat, stirring frequently, for 3–4 minutes, or until just softened.

Pour in the stock and stir in the carrots and potatoes. Bring to a boil, cover, and cook for 5 minutes.

Stir in the zucchini, tomatoes, lentils, kidney beans, and paprika and season to taste with salt and pepper. Bring to a boil, cover, and cook for 5 minutes.

Meanwhile, make the dumplings. Sift the flour, salt, baking powder, and paprika into a bowl. Stir in the herbs and suet. Bind together with the water to form a soft dough. Divide the dough into 8 portions and roll gently to form balls.

Uncover the stew, stir, then add the dumplings, pushing them slightly into the stew. Re-cover, reduce the heat so that the stew simmers, and cook for 15 minutes, or until the dumplings have risen and are cooked through.

Serve immediately on warmed plates, garnished with flat-leaf parsley.

spicy black-eye peas

serves 4

5–10 minutes,
plus 8 hours soaking

2 hours 15 minutes

2 cups dried black-eye peas, soaked
   overnight in cold water

1 tbsp vegetable oil

2 onions, chopped

1 tbsp clear honey

2 tbsp molasses

4 tbsp dark soy sauce

1 tsp mustard powder

4 tbsp tomato paste

2 cups vegetable stock

1 bay leaf

1 sprig each fresh rosemary, thyme,
   and sage

1 small orange

pepper

1 tbsp cornstarch

2 red bell peppers, seeded and diced

2 tbsp chopped fresh flatleaf parsley,
   to garnish

crusty bread, to serve

This is a hearty casserole of black-eye peas in a rich, sweet tomato sauce flavored with molasses and mustard.

Preheat the oven to 300°F/150°C. Rinse the beans and put into a pan. Cover with water, bring to a boil, and boil rapidly for 5 minutes. Drain and put into a casserole.

Meanwhile, heat the oil in a skillet. Add the onions and fry over low heat, stirring occasionally, for 5 minutes. Stir in the honey, molasses, soy sauce, mustard, and tomato paste. Pour in the stock, bring to a boil, and pour over the beans in the casserole.

Tie the bay leaf and herbs together with a clean piece of string and add to the casserole. Using a vegetable peeler, pare off 3 strips of orange rind and mix into the beans, along with plenty of pepper. Cover and cook in the preheated oven for 1 hour.

Squeeze the juice from the orange and blend with the cornstarch to form a smooth paste. Stir into the beans, together with the red bell peppers.

Cover the casserole and return to the oven for 1 hour, or until the sauce is rich and thick and the beans are very tender. Remove and discard the herbs and the orange rind.

Garnish with chopped parsley and serve immediately with crusty bread.

mixed bean pot

serves 4

10 minutes

about 1 hour

4 tbsp butter or margarine

1 large onion, chopped

2 garlic cloves, crushed

2 carrots, sliced

2 celery stalks, sliced

1 tbsp paprika

2 tsp ground cumin

14 oz/400 g canned chopped tomatoes

15 oz/425 g canned mixed beans, drained and rinsed

2/3 cup vegetable stock

1 tbsp raw sugar or molasses

12 oz/350 g mycoprotein (Quorn®) or soybean cubes

salt and pepper

crusty French bread, to serve

Cook this tasty vegetable and mycoprotein (Quorn®) casserole conventionally, then keep it piping hot until ready to serve.

variation

If you prefer, cook the casserole in a preheated oven at 375°F/190°C, but keep the dish covered. Instead of mixed beans, you could use just one type of canned beans.

Melt the butter or margarine in a large flameproof casserole and cook the onion and garlic over medium heat, stirring occasionally, for 5 minutes, or until golden brown.

Add the carrots and celery and cook, stirring occasionally, for an additional 2 minutes, then stir in the paprika and cumin.

Add the tomatoes and beans. Pour in the stock and add the sugar or molasses. Bring to a boil, then reduce the heat and simmer, uncovered, stirring occasionally, for 30 minutes.

Add the mycoprotein (Quorn®) or soybean cubes to the casserole, cover, and cook, stirring occasionally, for an additional 20 minutes.

Season to taste with salt and pepper, then keep the casserole very hot until ready to serve.

Ladle on to plates and serve with crusty French bread.

vegetable toad-in-the-hole

serves 4

5 minutes

about 55 minutes

batter
¾ cup all-purpose flour
pinch of salt
2 eggs, beaten
generous ¾ cup milk
2 tbsp whole-grain mustard
2 tbsp vegetable oil

filling
2 tbsp butter
2 garlic cloves, crushed

1 onion, cut into 8 wedges
2¾ oz/75 g baby carrots, halved
    lengthwise
1¾ oz/50 g green beans
1¾ oz/50 g canned corn, drained
2 tomatoes, seeded and cut
    into chunks
1 tsp whole-grain mustard
1 tbsp chopped fresh mixed herbs
salt and pepper

This dish can be cooked in a single large dish or in four individual pans.

Preheat the oven to 400°F/200°C. To make the batter, sift the flour and salt into a bowl. Beat in the eggs and milk to make a batter. Stir in the mustard and let stand.

Pour the oil into a shallow ovenproof dish and heat in the preheated oven for 10 minutes.

To make the filling, melt the butter in a skillet and sauté the garlic and onion, stirring constantly, for 2 minutes. Cook the carrots and beans in a pan of boiling water for 7 minutes, or until tender. Drain well.

Add the corn and tomatoes to the skillet with the mustard and chopped mixed herbs. Season well and add the carrots and beans.

Remove the heated dish from the oven and pour in the batter. Spoon the vegetables into the center, return to the oven, and cook for 30–35 minutes, or until the batter has risen and set. Serve immediately.

vegetable curry

serves 4

10 minutes

about 40 minutes

8 oz/225 g turnips or rutabaga
1 eggplant
12 oz/350 g new potatoes
8 oz/225 g cauliflower
8 oz/225 g white mushrooms
1 large onion
3 carrots
6 tbsp vegetable ghee or vegetable oil
2 garlic cloves, crushed
4 tsp finely chopped fresh gingerroot
1–2 fresh green chiles, seeded
    and chopped
1 tbsp paprika

2 tsp ground coriander
1 tbsp mild or medium curry powder
    or paste
2 cups vegetable stock
14 oz/400 g canned chopped
    tomatoes
salt
1 green bell pepper, seeded and
    sliced
1 tbsp cornstarch
2/3 cup coconut milk
2–3 tbsp ground almonds
fresh cilantro sprigs, to garnish

*This colorful and interesting
mixture of vegetables, cooked in
a spicy sauce, is excellent served
with rice and naan bread.*

Cut the turnips or rutabaga, eggplant, and potatoes into 1/2-inch/1-cm cubes. Divide the cauliflower into small florets. Leave the mushrooms whole or slice them thickly, if preferred. Slice the onion and carrots.

Heat the ghee or oil in a large pan. Add the onion, turnip or rutabaga, potato, and cauliflower and cook over low heat, stirring frequently, for 3 minutes.

Add the garlic, gingerroot, chiles, paprika, coriander, and curry powder or paste and cook, stirring, for 1 minute.

Add the stock, tomatoes, eggplant, and mushrooms and season to taste with salt. Cover and simmer, stirring occasionally, for 30 minutes, or until tender. Add the green bell pepper and carrots, cover, and cook for an additional 5 minutes.

Blend the cornstarch with the coconut milk to a smooth paste and stir into the mixture. Add the ground almonds and simmer, stirring constantly, for 2 minutes. Taste and adjust the seasoning, if necessary. Transfer to serving plates and serve hot, garnished with cilantro sprigs.

red curry with cashews

serves 4

5–10 minutes

about 15 minutes

generous 1 cup coconut milk

1 kaffir lime leaf

1/4 tsp light soy sauce

4 baby corn cobs, halved lengthwise

4 oz/115 g broccoli florets

4 oz/115 g green beans, cut into
   2-inch/5-cm pieces

4 tbsp cashew nuts

15 fresh basil leaves

1 tbsp chopped fresh cilantro

1 tbsp chopped roasted peanuts,
   to garnish

red curry paste

7 fresh red chiles, halved, seeded,
   and blanched

2 tsp cumin seeds

2 tsp coriander seeds

1-inch/2.5-cm piece galangal or fresh
   gingerroot, chopped

1/2 lemon grass stalk, chopped

1 tsp salt

grated rind of 1 lime

4 garlic cloves, chopped

3 shallots, chopped

2 kaffir lime leaves, shredded

1 tbsp vegetable oil

This is a wonderfully quick dish to prepare. If you don't have time to prepare the curry paste, it can be bought ready-made.

To make the curry paste, grind all the ingredients in a large mortar with a pestle or in a grinder. Alternatively, process briefly in a food processor. (The quantity of red curry paste is more than required for this recipe. Store for up to 3 weeks in a sealed jar in the refrigerator.)

Put a wok or large, heavy-bottomed skillet over high heat, add 3 table-spoons of the red curry paste, and stir until it gives off its aroma. Reduce the heat to medium.

Add the coconut milk, kaffir lime leaf, soy sauce, baby corn cobs, broccoli florets, green beans, and cashew nuts. Bring to a boil, then reduce the heat and simmer the curry for 10 minutes, or until the vegetables are cooked but still firm and crunchy.

Remove the lime leaf and stir in the basil leaves and cilantro. Transfer to a warmed serving dish, garnish with peanuts, and serve immediately.

potato & vegetable
curry

serves 4

5 minutes

45 minutes

4 tbsp vegetable oil

I lb 8 oz/675 g waxy potatoes,
cut into large chunks

2 onions, quartered

3 garlic cloves, crushed

I tsp garam masala

½ tsp ground turmeric

½ tsp ground cumin

½ tsp ground coriander

2 tsp grated fresh gingerroot

I fresh red chile, chopped

8 oz/225 g cauliflower florets

4 tomatoes, peeled and quartered

⅓ cup frozen peas

2 tbsp chopped fresh cilantro,
plus extra to garnish

I¼ cups vegetable stock

boiled rice or warm Indian bread,
to serve

*As meat is expensive in India
and much of the population
is vegetarian, Indian cuisine
abounds with tasty ways of
cooking with vegetables.*

cook's tip

*Use a large, heavy-bottomed
pan or skillet for this recipe to
ensure that the potatoes are
cooked thoroughly.*

Heat the oil in a large, heavy-bottomed pan or skillet. Add the potato chunks, onions, and garlic and fry over low heat, stirring frequently, for 2–3 minutes.

Add the garam masala, turmeric, cumin, coriander, gingerroot, and chile, mixing the spices into the vegetables until they are well coated. Fry over low heat, stirring constantly, for I minute.

Add the cauliflower florets, tomatoes, peas, chopped cilantro, and stock to the curry mixture.

Cook the potato curry over low heat for 30–40 minutes, or until the potatoes are tender and completely cooked through.

Serve the potato curry, garnished with fresh cilantro, with plain boiled rice or warm Indian bread.

mixed vegetable balti

serves 4

10 minutes

about 1 hour

generous 1 cup yellow split peas
3 tbsp vegetable oil
1 tsp onion seeds
2 onions, sliced
4 oz/115 g zucchini, sliced
4 oz/115 g potatoes, cut into
  1/2-inch/1-cm cubes
4 oz/115 g carrots, sliced
1 small eggplant, sliced

8 oz/225 g tomatoes, chopped
1 1/4 cups water
3 garlic cloves, chopped
1 tsp ground cumin
1 tsp ground coriander
1 tsp salt
2 fresh green chiles, sliced
1/2 tsp garam masala
2 tbsp chopped fresh cilantro

Any combination of vegetables or dried peas or beans can be used in this recipe. It would make a good dish for an informal vegetarian supper party.

Put the split peas into a pan and cover with lightly salted water. Bring to a boil, then reduce the heat and simmer for 30 minutes. Drain the peas and keep warm.

Heat the oil in a large skillet or wok, add the onion seeds, and fry until they start popping.

Add the onions and stir-fry over medium heat until golden brown.

Add the zucchini, potatoes, carrots, and eggplant. Stir-fry the vegetables for about 2 minutes.

Stir in the tomatoes, water, garlic, cumin, coriander, salt, chiles, garam masala, and reserved split peas.

Bring to a boil, then reduce the heat and simmer for 15 minutes, or until all the vegetables are tender.

Stir the fresh cilantro into the vegetables. Transfer to a warmed serving dish and serve immediately.

sweet & sour eggplants

serves 4

5–10 minutes, plus
30 minutes standing

about 30 minutes

2 large eggplants
6 tbsp olive oil
4 garlic cloves, crushed
1 onion, cut into 8 wedges
4 large tomatoes,
    seeded and chopped
3 tbsp chopped fresh mint

2/3 cup vegetable stock
4 tsp brown sugar
2 tbsp red wine vinegar
1 tsp dried chili flakes
salt and pepper
fresh mint sprigs, to garnish

This is a dish of Persian origin, not Chinese as it sounds. Eggplants are fried and mixed with tomatoes, mint, sugar, and vinegar for a really intense flavor.

cook's tip

Mint is a popular herb in Middle Eastern cooking. It is a useful herb to grow yourself as it can be added to a variety of dishes, particularly salads and vegetable dishes. It can be grown easily in a garden or window box.

Using a sharp knife, cut the eggplants into cubes. Put them into a colander, sprinkle with salt, and let stand for 30 minutes. Rinse thoroughly under cold running water and drain well. This process removes all the bitter juices from the eggplants. Pat dry with paper towels.

Heat the oil in a large skillet and sauté the eggplants, stirring constantly, for 1–2 minutes.

Stir in the garlic and onion and cook for an additional 2–3 minutes.

Stir in the tomatoes, mint, and stock, cover, and cook for 15–20 minutes, or until the vegetables are tender.

Stir in the sugar, vinegar, and dried chili flakes, season to taste with salt and pepper, and cook for 2–3 minutes. Garnish the eggplants with mint sprigs and serve.

vegetable chili

serves 4

5 minutes

about 1 hour 10 minutes

1 eggplant, peeled if wished, cut into 1-inch/2.5-cm slices

1 tbsp olive oil, plus extra for brushing

1 large red or yellow onion, finely chopped

2 red or yellow bell peppers, seeded and finely chopped

3–4 garlic cloves, finely chopped or crushed

1 lb 12 oz/800 g canned chopped tomatoes

1 tbsp mild chili powder

½ tsp ground cumin

½ tsp dried oregano

salt and pepper

2 small zucchini, quartered lengthwise and sliced

14 oz/400 g canned kidney beans, drained and rinsed

2 cups water

1 tbsp tomato paste

6 scallions, finely chopped

1 cup grated Cheddar cheese

This is a hearty and flavorful dish that is good on its own or spooned over cooked rice or baked potatoes for a more substantial meal.

Brush the eggplant slices on one side with oil. Heat half the oil in a large, heavy-bottomed skillet over medium–high heat. Add the eggplant slices, oiled-side up, and cook for 5–6 minutes, or until browned on one side. Turn the slices over, cook on the other side until browned, and transfer to a plate. Cut into bite-size pieces.

Heat the remaining oil in a large pan over medium heat. Add the onion and bell peppers and cook, stirring occasionally, for 3–4 minutes, or until the onion is just softened but not browned. Add the garlic and continue cooking for 2–3 minutes, or until the onion is just beginning to color.

Add the tomatoes, chili powder, cumin, and oregano. Season to taste with salt and pepper. Bring just to a boil, then reduce the heat, cover, and simmer gently for 15 minutes.

Add the sliced zucchini, eggplant pieces, and kidney beans. Stir in the water and the tomato paste. Return to a boil, then cover the pan and continue simmering for 45 minutes, or until the vegetables are tender. Taste and then adjust the seasoning, if necessary. If you prefer a hotter dish, stir in a little more chili powder.

Ladle into warmed bowls and top with chopped scallions and cheese.

easy cheese risotto

serves 4–6

5 minutes

35 minutes

4–6 tbsp unsalted butter
1 onion, finely chopped
1 1/2 cups risotto rice
1/2 cup dry white vermouth
  or white wine

1 quart chicken or vegetable stock,
  simmering
3/4 cup freshly grated Parmesan
  cheese, plus extra for sprinkling
salt and pepper

Although this is the easiest, most basic risotto, it is one of the most delicious. Because there are few ingredients, use the best of each.

cook's tip

If you prefer not to use butter, soften the onion in 2 tablespoons olive oil and stir in about 2 tablespoons extra virgin olive oil with the Parmesan at the end.

Heat about 2 tablespoons of the butter in a large, heavy-bottomed pan over medium heat. Add the onion and cook for 2 minutes, or until just beginning to soften. Add the rice and cook, stirring frequently, for 2 minutes, or until translucent and well coated with the butter.

Pour in the vermouth or wine; it will bubble and steam rapidly and evaporate almost immediately. Add a ladleful (about 1 cup) of the simmering stock and cook, stirring constantly, until the stock is completely absorbed.

Continue adding the stock, about half a ladleful at a time, allowing each addition to be absorbed before adding the next—never allow the rice to cook "dry". This should take 20–25 minutes. The risotto should have a creamy consistency and the rice grains should be tender but still firm to the bite.

Switch off the heat and stir in the remaining butter and Parmesan cheese. Season to taste with salt and pepper. Cover, let stand for about 1 minute, then serve with extra Parmesan cheese for sprinkling.

sun-dried
tomato risotto

serves 4

10 minutes

about 35 minutes

1 tbsp olive oil
2 tbsp butter
1 large onion, finely chopped
1²/3 cups risotto rice, washed
about 15 saffron strands
²/3 cup white wine

3¹/2 cups hot vegetable or chicken stock
8 sun-dried tomatoes, cut into strips
scant 1 cup frozen peas, thawed
2³/4 oz/75 g Parmesan cheese, grated, plus extra to serve

A Milanese risotto can be cooked in a variety of ways—but always with saffron. This version with sun-dried tomatoes and wine has a lovely tangy flavor.

variation

For a non-vegetarian alternative, try adding shredded prosciutto with peas and Parmesan cheese.

Heat the oil and butter in a large skillet. Add the onion and cook for 4–5 minutes, or until softened.

Add the rice and saffron to the pan, stirring well to coat the rice in the oil, and cook for 1 minute.

Add the wine and stock slowly to the rice mixture in the pan, a ladleful at a time, stirring and making sure that all the liquid is absorbed before adding the next ladleful of liquid.

About halfway through adding the stock, stir in the sun-dried tomatoes.

When all of the wine and stock is incorporated, the rice should be cooked. Test by tasting a grain—if it is still crunchy, add a little more water and continue cooking. It should take about 20–25 minutes to cook.

Stir in the peas and Parmesan cheese. Cook for 2–3 minutes, stirring, until hot. Serve with extra grated Parmesan cheese.

exotic mushroom risotto

serves 4

5–10 minutes,
plus 30 minutes soaking

about 30 minutes

2 oz/55 g dried porcini (cèpes) or
　morel mushrooms

about 1 lb 2 oz/500 g mixed fresh
　exotic mushrooms, halved if large

4 tbsp olive oil

3–4 garlic cloves, finely chopped

4 tbsp unsalted butter

1 onion, finely chopped

1 3/4 cups arborio or carnaroli rice

4 tbsp dry white vermouth

1 quart chicken stock, simmering

salt and pepper

1 cup freshly grated Parmesan cheese

4 tbsp chopped fresh flatleaf parsley

*Distinctive-tasting exotic
mushrooms, so popular in
Italy, give this aromatic risotto
a wonderful, robust flavor.*

Put the dried mushrooms into a bowl and add boiling water to cover. Set aside to soak for 30 minutes, then carefully lift out and pat dry. Strain the soaking liquid through a strainer lined with paper towels and set aside.

Trim the exotic mushrooms and gently brush clean.

Heat 3 tablespoons of the oil in a large skillet. Add the fresh mushrooms and stir-fry for 1–2 minutes. Add the garlic and the soaked mushrooms and cook, stirring frequently, for 2 minutes. Transfer to a plate.

Heat the remaining oil and half the butter in a large heavy-bottomed pan. Add the onion and cook, stirring occasionally, for 2 minutes, or until softened. Add the rice and cook, stirring frequently, for 2 minutes, or until translucent and well coated.

Add the vermouth. When almost absorbed, add a ladleful (about 1 cup) of the stock. Cook, stirring constantly, until the liquid is absorbed.

Continue adding the stock, about half a ladleful at a time, allowing each addition to be completely absorbed before adding the next. This should take 20–25 minutes. The risotto should have a creamy consistency and the rice should be tender but still firm to the bite.

Add half the reserved mushroom soaking liquid to the risotto and stir in the mushrooms. Season to taste with salt and pepper and add more mushroom liquid, if necessary. Remove the pan from the heat and stir in the remaining butter, the grated Parmesan cheese, and chopped parsley. Serve immediately.

roasted pumpkin risotto

serves 6

5 minutes

about 35 minutes

4 tbsp olive oil

4 tbsp unsalted butter, diced

1 lb/450 g pumpkin flesh, cut into ½-inch/1-cm dice

large sprig fresh sage

2 garlic cloves, finely chopped

salt and pepper

2 tbsp lemon juice

2 large shallots, finely chopped

1²/₃ cups risotto rice

4 tbsp dry white vermouth

1 quart chicken stock, simmering

½ cup freshly grated Parmesan cheese

10½ oz/300 g Gorgonzola cheese, diced

celery leaves, to garnish

The combination of sweet creamy pumpkin with the saltiness of Gorgonzola cheese and the pungency of sage is delicious.

Preheat the oven to 400°F/200°C. Put half the oil and about 1 tablespoon of the butter in a roasting pan and heat in the preheated oven.

When the butter has melted, arrange the pumpkin in the pan and sprinkle with the sage, half the garlic, and salt and pepper to taste. Toss together and roast for 10 minutes, or until just softened and beginning to caramelize. Transfer the pumpkin to a plate.

Roughly mash about half the cooked pumpkin with the lemon juice and reserve with the remaining diced pumpkin.

Heat the remaining oil and 1 tablespoon of the remaining butter in a large, heavy-bottomed pan over medium heat. Add the shallots and remaining garlic and cook, stirring occasionally, for about 1 minute. Add the rice and cook, stirring constantly, for 2 minutes, or until well coated.

Pour in the vermouth; it will bubble and steam rapidly. Add a ladleful (about 1 cup) of the simmering stock and cook, stirring constantly, until the stock is absorbed.

Continue adding the stock, about half a ladleful at a time, allowing each addition to be absorbed before adding the next—never allow the rice to cook "dry". This should take 20–25 minutes. The risotto should have a creamy consistency and the rice should be tender but still firm to the bite.

Stir all the pumpkin into the risotto with the remaining butter and the Parmesan cheese. Remove from the heat and fold in the Gorgonzola. Serve the risotto immediately, garnished with celery leaves.

baked tomato rice

serves 4

5 minutes

about 45 minutes

2 tbsp vegetable oil

1 onion, coarsely chopped

1 red bell pepper, seeded and chopped

2 garlic cloves, finely chopped

½ tsp dried thyme

1½ cups long-grain rice

4 cups chicken or vegetable stock

8 oz/225 g canned chopped tomatoes

1 bay leaf

2 tbsp shredded fresh basil

6 oz/175 g sharp Cheddar cheese, grated

2 tbsp snipped fresh chives

4 herbed pork sausages, cooked and cut into ½-inch/1-cm pieces

2–3 tbsp freshly grated Parmesan cheese

A great quick supper for the family, this dish is incredibly simple to put together, yet is truly scrumptious!

variation

For a vegetarian version, replace the pork sausages with 14 oz/400 g canned drained lima beans, kidney beans, or corn. Alternatively, try a mixture of sautéed mushrooms and zucchini.

Preheat the oven to 350°F/180°C. Heat the vegetable oil in a large flameproof casserole over medium heat. Add the onion and red bell pepper and cook, stirring frequently, for 5 minutes, or until soft and lightly colored. Stir in the garlic and thyme and cook for an additional minute.

Add the rice and cook, stirring frequently, for 2 minutes, or until the rice is well coated and translucent. Stir in the stock, tomatoes, and bay leaf. Bring to a boil and simmer vigorously for 5 minutes until the stock is almost completely absorbed.

Stir in the basil, Cheddar cheese, chives, and sausages, cover, and cook in the preheated oven for about 25 minutes.

Sprinkle with the Parmesan cheese and return to the oven, uncovered, for 5 minutes, or until the top is golden. Serve hot, straight from the casserole.

kitchouri

serves 4

10 minutes

about 30 minutes

2 tbsp pure or vegetable ghee, or butter

I red onion, finely chopped

I garlic clove, crushed

1/2 celery stalk, finely chopped

I tsp ground turmeric

1/2 tsp garam masala

I fresh green chile, seeded and finely chopped

1/2 tsp cumin seeds

I tbsp chopped fresh cilantro

2/3 cup basmati rice, rinsed under cold water

2/3 cup green lentils

1 1/4 cups vegetable juice

2 1/2 cups vegetable stock

The traditional breakfast dish, kedgeree, reputedly has its roots in this Indian flavored rice dish.

cook's tip

This is a versatile dish, and can also be served as a winter lunch dish with tomatoes and yogurt.

Heat the ghee or butter in a large, heavy-bottomed pan. Add the onion, garlic, and celery to the pan and cook for 5 minutes, or until soft.

Add the turmeric, garam masala, chopped green chile, cumin seeds, and cilantro. Cook over medium heat, stirring constantly, for 1 minute, or until fragrant.

Add the rice and lentils and cook for 1 minute, until the rice is translucent.

Pour the vegetable juice and stock into the pan and bring to a boil over medium heat. Cover and simmer over low heat, stirring occasionally, for 20 minutes, or until the lentils are cooked (they should be tender when pressed between 2 fingers).

Transfer the kitchouri to a warmed serving dish and serve piping hot.

cashew nut paella

serves 4

15 minutes

30 minutes

2 tbsp olive oil

1 tbsp butter

1 red onion, chopped

3/4 cup risotto rice

1 tsp ground turmeric

1 tsp ground cumin

1/2 tsp chili powder

3 garlic cloves, crushed

1 fresh green chile, sliced

1 green bell pepper, seeded and diced

1 red bell pepper, seeded and diced

2 3/4 oz/75 g baby corn cobs, halved lengthwise

2 tbsp pitted black olives

1 large tomato, seeded and diced

generous 1 3/4 cups vegetable stock

1/2 cup unsalted cashew nuts

1/4 cup frozen peas, thawed

salt and pepper

chopped fresh parsley and cayenne pepper, for sprinkling

Paella traditionally contains chicken and fish, but this recipe is packed with vegetables and nuts for a truly delicious and simple vegetarian dish.

cook's tip

For authenticity and flavor, use a few saffron strands soaked in a little boiling water instead of the turmeric. Saffron has a lovely, nutty flavor.

Heat the oil and butter in a large skillet or paella pan until the butter has melted.

Add the chopped onion to the pan and sauté, stirring for 2–3 minutes, or until the onion has softened.

Stir in the rice, turmeric, cumin, chili powder, garlic, chile, bell peppers, corn cobs, olives, and tomato and cook over medium heat for 1–2 minutes, stirring occasionally.

Pour in the stock and bring the mixture to a boil. Reduce the heat and cook for 20 minutes, stirring.

Add the cashew nuts and peas to the mixture in the pan and cook for an additional 5 minutes, stirring occasionally. Season to taste with salt and pepper and sprinkle with parsley and cayenne pepper. Transfer to warmed serving plates and serve immediately.

vegetable jambalaya

serves 4

5 minutes

1 hour

generous 1/3 cup brown rice (see
  Cook's Tip)
2 tbsp olive oil
2 garlic cloves, crushed
1 red onion, cut into 8 wedges
1 eggplant, diced
1 green bell pepper, seeded and diced
2 oz/55 g baby corn cobs,
  halved lengthwise

scant 1/2 cup frozen peas
3 1/2 oz/100 g small broccoli florets
2/3 cup vegetable stock
8 oz/225 g canned chopped tomatoes
1 tbsp tomato paste
1 tsp creole seasoning
1/2 tsp dried chili flakes
salt and pepper

*This spicy rice dish is a vegetarian
version of the traditional jambalaya.
Packed with a variety of vegetables,
it is both colorful and nutritious.*

cook's tip

*Use a mixture of different kinds of
rice, such as wild or red rice, to add
color and texture to this dish. Cook
the rice in advance, following the
instructions on the package, for
a speedier recipe.*

Cook the rice in a large pan of salted boiling water for 20 minutes, or until
cooked through. Drain the rice, rinse with boiling water, drain again, and
set aside.

Heat the oil in a heavy-bottomed skillet and cook the garlic and onion,
stirring constantly, for 2–3 minutes. Add the eggplant, bell pepper, corn
cobs, peas, and broccoli to the pan and cook, stirring occasionally, for an
additional 2–3 minutes.

Stir in the stock and the canned tomatoes, tomato paste, creole seasoning,
and dried chili flakes.

Season to taste with salt and pepper and cook over low heat for 15–20
minutes, or until the vegetables are tender.

Stir the brown rice into the vegetable mixture and cook, mixing well, for
3–4 minutes, or until hot.

Transfer the jambalaya to a warmed serving dish and serve at once.

desserts

For many cooks dessert is one course too far, but for most diners it is a fine finale to a meal. Compromise with this delightful selection of one-pot sweet dishes. Why bother with a conventional—and boring—fruit pie when, with far less effort and washing-up, you could make Clafoutis (see page 232), a melt-in-the-mouth combination of succulent cherries and crispy batter, or Tarte Tatin (see page 220), an all-in-one upside-down apple pie?

Whatever the season and whatever the occasion, you will find the perfect dish to round off your meal—whether an alfresco lunch, a midwinter supper, or a sophisticated dinner party. There are lots of child-friendly treats for family suppers, from Crêpe Pieces (see page 234) to Apple Fritters (see page 236), as well as some delicious dishes for the more adult palate, from Zabaglione (see page 240) to liqueur-laced Warm Currants in Cassis (see page 244). Fruit features in many forms—Fall Fruit Bread Pudding (see page 230) contrasts with Exotic Fruit Pockets (see page 254). There are light, summery desserts along with comforting, substantial dishes, to make sure that even the heartiest appetite is finally satisfied.

tarte tatin

serves 4

10–15 minutes,
plus 30 minutes chilling

about 1 hour 5 minutes

8 oz/225 g unsweetened pastry,
  thawed if frozen
all-purpose flour, for dusting
10 eating apples, such as
  Golden Delicious

4 tbsp lemon juice
½ cup unsalted butter,
  diced
scant ⅔ cup superfine sugar
½ tsp ground cinnamon

This upside-down apple tart has been a specialty of Sologne in the Loire valley for centuries, but was made famous by the Tatin sisters who ran a hotel-restaurant in Lamotte-Beuvron at the beginning of the twentieth century.

Preheat the oven to 450°F/230°C. Roll out the pastry dough on a lightly floured work surface into a ¼-inch/5-mm thick round, about 11 inches/28 cm in diameter. Transfer to a lightly floured cookie sheet and let chill in the refrigerator for 30 minutes.

Peel, halve, and core the apples, then brush with the lemon juice to prevent any discoloration. Heat the butter, sugar, and cinnamon in a 10-inch/25-cm tarte tatin pan or heavy-bottomed skillet with a flameproof handle over low heat, stirring occasionally, until the butter has melted and the sugar has dissolved. Cook for an additional 6–8 minutes, or until the mixture is a light caramel color. Remove from the heat.

Arrange the apples in the pan or skillet, packing them in tightly. Return to the heat and cook for 25 minutes, or until the apples are tender and lightly colored. Remove from the heat and let cool slightly.

Place the pastry over the apples, tucking in the edges. Prick the top and bake in the preheated oven for 30 minutes, or until golden. Let cool slightly, then run a knife around the edge of the pan to loosen the pastry. Invert on to a plate and serve warm.

one roll fruit pie

serves 4

10–15 minutes, plus
30 minutes chilling

35 minutes

dough

scant 1¼ cups all-purpose flour

scant ½ cup butter, cut into small
pieces, plus extra for greasing

1 tbsp water

1 egg, separated

sugar lumps, crushed, for sprinkling

filling

1 lb 5 oz/600 g prepared fruit
(rhubarb, plums, or damsons)

scant ½ cup brown sugar

1 tbsp ground ginger

*This is an easy way to make a pie:
once you have rolled out the dough
and filled it with fruit, you just turn
the edges of the dough in!*

cook's tip

*If the pastry breaks when shaping
it into a round, don't panic—just
patch and seal, as the overall
effect of this pie is rough.*

Grease a large cookie sheet with a little butter.

To make the dough, put the flour and butter into a mixing bowl and rub in the butter with your fingertips until the mixture resembles bread crumbs. Add the water and work the mixture together until a soft dough has formed. Wrap and chill in the refrigerator for 30 minutes.

Preheat the oven to 400°F/200°C. On a lightly floured surface, roll out the chilled dough to a round about 14 inches/35 cm in diameter.

Transfer the round to the center of the greased cookie sheet. Brush the dough with the egg yolk.

To make the filling, mix the prepared fruit with the sugar and ginger and pile it into the center of the dough.

Turn in the edges of the dough all the way around. Brush the surface of the dough with the egg white and sprinkle with the crushed sugar lumps.

Bake in the preheated oven for 35 minutes, or until golden brown. Transfer to a serving plate and serve warm.

italian bread pudding

serves 4

5–10 minutes, plus 30 minutes soaking

25 minutes

1 tbsp butter

2 small eating apples, peeled, cored, and sliced into rings

scant ½ cup granulated sugar

2 tbsp white wine

4 thick slices bread (about 4 oz/ 115 g), crusts removed (day-old baguette is ideal)

1¼ cups light cream

2 eggs, beaten

pared rind of 1 orange, cut into short thin sticks

This deliciously rich pudding is cooked with cream and apples and is delicately flavored with orange.

Lightly grease a 1-quart deep ovenproof dish with the butter.

Arrange the apple rings in the bottom of the dish. Sprinkle half of the sugar over the apples.

Pour the wine over the apples. Add the bread slices, pushing them down with your hands to flatten them slightly.

Mix the cream with the eggs, the remaining sugar, and the orange rind and pour the mixture over the bread. Let soak for 30 minutes. Preheat the oven to 350°F/180°C.

Bake in the preheated oven for 25 minutes, or until golden and set. Remove the pudding from the oven, let cool slightly, and serve warm.

spiced steamed pudding

serves 6

about 15 minutes

1 hour 30 minutes

2 tbsp corn syrup, plus extra to serve

generous 1/2 cup butter or margarine, plus extra for greasing

2/3 cup superfine or brown sugar

2 eggs

scant 1 1/4 cups self-rising flour

3/4 tsp ground cinnamon or allspice

grated rind of 1 orange

1 tbsp orange juice

1/2 cup golden raisins

1 1/2 oz/40 g preserved ginger, finely chopped

1 eating apple, peeled, cored, and coarsely grated

Steamed puddings are irresistible on a winter's day, but the texture of this pudding is so light it can be served throughout the year.

Thoroughly grease a 3 1/2-cup ovenproof bowl. Put the corn syrup into the bowl.

Cream the butter or margarine and sugar together until very light and fluffy and pale in color. Beat in the eggs, one at a time, following each with a spoonful of the flour.

Sift the remaining flour with the cinnamon or allspice and fold into the mixture, followed by the orange rind and juice. Fold in the golden raisins, then the ginger and apple.

Turn the mixture into the ovenproof bowl and level the top. Cover with a piece of pleated greased parchment paper, tucking the edges under the rim of the bowl.

Cover with a sheet of pleated foil. Tie securely in place with string, with a piece of string tied over the top of the bowl for a handle to make it easy to lift out of the pan.

Put the bowl into a pan half-filled with boiling water, cover, and steam for 1 1/2 hours, adding more boiling water to the pan as necessary during cooking.

To serve, remove the foil and paper, turn the pudding out on to a warmed serving plate, and serve at once in slices with extra corn syrup.

indian rice pudding

serves 4

10 minutes

30 minutes

generous ⅓ cup basmati rice
1 quart milk
8 tbsp sugar

varq (silver leaf) or chopped
pistachios, to decorate

*Indian rice pudding is
cooked in a pan over low
heat, rather than in the oven
like the British version.*

cook's tip

*Varq is edible silver leaf which is
used to decorate elaborate dishes
prepared for special occasions and
celebrations in India. It is pure silver
that has been beaten until it is
wafer-thin. It comes with a backing
paper that is peeled off as the varq
is laid on the cooked food.*

Rinse the rice and put into a large pan. Add half the milk and bring to a boil over very low heat.

Cook, stirring occasionally, until the milk has been completely absorbed by the rice.

Remove the pan from the heat. Mash the rice, making swift, round movements in the pan, for at least 5 minutes, or until all of the lumps have been removed.

Gradually add the remaining milk. Bring to a boil again over low heat, stirring occasionally.

Add the sugar and continue to cook, stirring constantly, for 7–10 minutes, or until the mixture is quite thick in consistency.

Transfer the rice pudding to a heatproof serving bowl. Decorate with varq (silver leaf) or chopped pistachios and serve on its own or with pooris.

fall fruit bread pudding

serves 8

15 minutes, plus
8 hours chilling

15 minutes

2 lb/900 g mixed blackberries,
   chopped apples, and chopped
   pears
generous ¾ cup brown sugar
1 tsp ground cinnamon

7 tbsp water
8 oz/225 g white bread, thickly sliced
   (about 12 slices), crusts removed

This is like a summer pudding, but it uses fruits that appear later in the year. This dessert requires chilling overnight, so prepare in advance.

cook's tip

This pudding would be delicious served with vanilla ice cream to counteract the tartness of the blackberries. Stand the pudding on a plate when chilling to catch any juices that run down the sides of the bowl.

Put the fruit into a large pan with the sugar, cinnamon, and water, stir, and bring to a boil. Reduce the heat and simmer for 5–10 minutes so that the fruits soften but still hold their shape.

Meanwhile, line the bottom and sides of a 3½-cup ovenproof bowl with the bread slices, ensuring that there are no gaps between the pieces of bread.

Spoon the fruit into the center of the bread-lined bowl and cover the fruit with the remaining bread.

Put a saucer on top of the bread pudding and put a heavy weight on the saucer. Chill the pudding in the refrigerator overnight.

Turn the pudding out on to a serving plate and serve immediately.

clafoutis

serves 4

15 minutes, plus
1 hour standing

45 minutes

1 lb/450 g sweet black cherries
2 tbsp cherry brandy
1 tbsp confectioner's sugar, plus
   extra for dusting
butter, for greasing

batter

3 tbsp all-purpose flour
3 tbsp sugar
¾ cup light cream
2 eggs, lightly beaten
grated rind of ½ lemon
¼ tsp vanilla extract

Although the many different recipes for this unusual batter-based dessert may use a variety of fruits, cherries are the classic filling in the Limousin in France, where the dish originated.

cook's tip

Traditionally, in the Limousin, the cherries are not pitted before cooking, because the pits are thought to release extra flavor into the dessert.

Preheat the oven to 375°F/190°C. Pit the cherries, then put into a bowl with the cherry brandy and confectioner's sugar and mix together. Cover with plastic wrap and let stand for 1 hour.

Meanwhile, grease a shallow, ovenproof dish with butter. To make the batter, sift the flour into a bowl and stir in the sugar. Gradually whisk in the cream, beaten eggs, lemon rind, and vanilla extract. Whisk constantly until the batter is completely smooth.

Spoon the cherries into the ovenproof dish and pour the batter over them to cover. Bake in the preheated oven for 45 minutes, or until golden and set. Lightly dust with extra confectioner's sugar and serve warm, or let cool to room temperature before serving.

crêpe pieces

serves 4

5 minutes

about 10 minutes

2 tbsp superfine sugar
1 tsp ground cinnamon
scant 1 cup all-purpose flour
pinch of salt
2 eggs, lightly beaten

½ cup milk
14 oz/400 g canned apricot
  halves in syrup
corn oil, for brushing

This is a cheap and cheerful, easy-to-make dessert that is perfect for midweek family suppers, and surprisingly filling. Its casual presentation makes it a favorite with children.

cook's tip

Before you add the batter to the skillet, make sure the oil is very hot. Tilt and roll the pan as you pour the batter in, to spread it over the bottom in a thin layer.

Put the sugar and cinnamon into a bowl, stir to mix, and reserve. Sift the flour and salt into a separate bowl. Whisk the eggs and milk into the flour and continue whisking to make a smooth batter.

Drain the apricot halves, reserving the syrup, then whisk the syrup into the batter until combined. Coarsely chop the apricots and reserve.

Heat a large crêpe pan or heavy-bottomed skillet and brush with oil. Pour in the batter and cook over medium heat for 4–5 minutes, or until the underside is golden brown. Turn over with a spatula or palette knife and cook the second side for 4 minutes, or until golden. Tear the crêpe into bite-size pieces with 2 spoons or forks.

Add the apricots to the pan and heat through briefly. Divide the crêpe pieces and apricots among individual plates, sprinkle with the sugar and cinnamon mixture, and serve immediately.

apple fritters

serves 4

5–10 minutes, plus
30 minutes standing

10–15 minutes

generous ¾ cup all-purpose flour
pinch of salt
2 egg yolks
1 egg white
1 tbsp corn oil
⅔ cup milk

1 lb/450 g cooking apples
juice of 1 lemon
superfine sugar, for sprinkling
½ cup unsalted butter
plain yogurt, to serve

This is a very popular choice for family meals, as children and adults alike love the flavor and crispy texture of the apple rings—and you don't need a spoon or fork to eat them.

cook's tip

Choose firm, tart apples for this dish. Once they are cut, they should be sprinkled with lemon juice immediately and cooked quickly to prevent any discoloration.

Sift the flour and salt into a mixing bowl. Make a well in the center and add the egg yolks, egg white, and oil. Gradually incorporate the flour into the liquid with a wooden spoon. Gradually beat in the milk and continue beating to make a smooth batter. Cover with plastic wrap and let stand for 30 minutes.

Peel and core the apples, then cut them into rings about ¼-inch/5-mm thick. Spread them out on a plate and sprinkle with the lemon juice and a little sugar.

Melt the butter in a large, heavy-bottomed skillet over medium heat. Dip the apple rings into the batter, one at a time, then drop them into the pan. Cook for 2–3 minutes on each side, or until golden. Transfer to a serving platter, sprinkle with sugar, and serve with yogurt.

fruit brûlée

serves 4

5 minutes, plus 1 hour 10 minutes cooling and chilling

about 15 minutes

4 plums, pitted and sliced
2 cooking apples, peeled and sliced
1 tsp ground ginger
2½ cups strained plain yogurt

2 tbsp confectioner's sugar, sifted
1 tsp almond essence
scant ½ cup raw brown sugar

This is a cheat's brûlée, in that yogurt is used to cover a base of fruits, before being sprinkled with sugar and grilled.

Put the plums and apples into a pan with 2 tablespoons of water and cook for 7–10 minutes, or until tender but not mushy. Let cool for 10 minutes, then stir in the ground ginger.

Using a perforated spoon, spoon the mixture into the bottom of a shallow, ovenproof serving dish.

Combine the yogurt, confectioner's sugar, and almond essence and spoon over the fruits to cover.

Sprinkle the brown sugar over the top of the yogurt and cook under a preheated hot broiler for 3–4 minutes, or until the sugar has melted and formed a crust.

Let chill in the refrigerator for 1 hour before serving.

zabaglione

serves 4

10 minutes

10 minutes

5 egg yolks
½ cup superfine sugar

⅔ cup Marsala or sweet sherry
fresh fruit or amaretti cookies,
to serve (optional)

This well-known dish is a light but rich mousse flavored with Marsala. It will not keep, so make it fresh and serve immediately.

cook's tip

Any other type of liqueur may be used instead of the Marsala, or sweet sherry, if you prefer. Serve soft fruits such as strawberries or raspberries with the zabaglione to make a delicious combination.

Put the egg yolks into a large mixing bowl.

Add the sugar to the egg yolks and whisk them together until the mixture is thick and very pale and has doubled in volume.

Put the bowl containing the whisked egg yolks and sugar over a pan of gently simmering water.

Add the Marsala or sweet sherry to the egg yolk and sugar mixture and continue whisking until the foam mixture becomes warm. This process may take as long as 10 minutes.

Pour the mixture, which should be frothy and light, into 4 wine glasses.

Serve the zabaglione warm with fresh fruits or amaretti cookies.

oranges & strawberries

serves 4

15 minutes

–

3 sweet oranges
8 oz/225 g strawberries
grated rind and juice of 1 lime

1–2 tbsp superfine sugar
1 fresh mint sprig, to decorate

Ideal as a summery dessert, this dish can also be served as a fresh fruit dish with brunch. The oranges enhance the delicate flavor of the berries.

variation

An optional hint of orange-flavored liqueur is delicious on this—reduce or omit the sugar. You can replace the oranges with mangoes, and the strawberries with blackberries, for a dramatically colored dessert.

Using a sharp knife, cut a slice off the top and bottom of the oranges, then remove the peel and all the pith, cutting downward and taking care to retain the shape of the oranges.

Using a small, sharp knife, cut down between the membranes of the oranges to remove the segments. Discard the membranes.

Hull the strawberries, pulling the leaves off with a pinching action. Cut into slices, along the length of the strawberries.

Put the oranges and strawberries into a bowl, then sprinkle with the lime rind, lime juice, and sugar. Chill in the refrigerator until ready to serve.

To serve, transfer to a serving bowl and decorate the dish with mint.

warm currants in cassis

serves 4

5–10 minutes

10 minutes

3 cups black currants
2 cups red currants
4 tbsp superfine sugar
grated rind and juice of 1 orange

2 tsp arrowroot
2 tbsp crème de cassis
whipped cream or lowfat plain
   yogurt, to serve

Crème de cassis is a black currant-based liqueur which comes from France and is an excellent flavoring for fruit dishes.

Using a fork, strip the black currants and red currants from their stems and put into a pan.

Add the sugar and orange rind and juice and heat gently, stirring, until the sugar has dissolved. Bring the fruit mixture to a boil and simmer gently for 5 minutes.

Strain the currants and put into a bowl, then return the juice to the pan.

Blend the arrowroot with a little water and mix into the juice in the pan. Boil the mixture until thickened.

Let cool slightly, then stir in the crème de cassis and poor over the fruits.

Serve the fruits in individual dishes with whipped cream or yogurt.

caramelized oranges

serves 4

10–15 minutes, plus
2 hours chilling

about 20 minutes

6 large oranges
5 tbsp water
½ cup superfine sugar
whipped cream, to serve

These unusual, sugar-coated oranges look almost too pretty to eat—but make sure you do, because they taste wonderfully refreshing, with a real citrus tang.

cook's tip

For recipes using citrus rind, look for unwaxed specimens—that is, those that have not been treated with diphenyl to preserve their color.

Carefully pare wide strips of rind from 2 of the oranges using a swivel-blade vegetable peeler. Cut the strips of rind into thin sticks with a sharp knife and reserve a few for decoration. Peel all the oranges and remove traces of white pith. Cut the fruits horizontally into slices ½ inch/1 cm thick. Put into a serving bowl and tip in any spilt juice.

Before making the caramel, half-fill the sink with cold water. Put 3 table-spoons of water and all of the sugar into a heavy-bottomed pan and bring to a boil, stirring constantly until the sugar has dissolved. Boil, without stirring, until the syrup is a dark caramel color. Remove the pan from the heat and carefully immerse the bottom in the cold water to prevent any further cooking.

Add the remaining 2 tablespoons of water to the pan with the orange rind and simmer over low heat, stirring occasionally, for 8–10 minutes, or until the rind is almost translucent. Pour the mixture over the orange slices, turning them to coat. Cool completely, then chill the oranges in the refrigerator for 1–2 hours. Serve with whipped cream, decorated with orange rind.

baked apples
with berries

serves 4

5–10 minutes

45–50 minutes

4 tart cooking apples

1 tbsp lemon juice

²/₃ cup prepared blackberries, thawed
   if frozen

½ oz/15 g slivered almonds

½ tsp allspice

½ tsp finely grated lemon rind

2 tbsp raw brown sugar

1¼ cups ruby port

1 cinnamon stick, broken

2 tsp cornstarch blended with 2 tbsp
   cold water

lowfat custard, to serve

*This winter dessert is
a classic dish. Large, fluffy
apples are hollowed out
and filled with spices,
almonds, and blackberries.*

Preheat the oven to 400°F/200°C. Wash and dry the apples. Using a small, sharp knife, make a shallow cut through the skin around the middle of each apple—this will prevent the apples from bursting during cooking.

Core the apples, brush the centers with the lemon juice to prevent them from browning, and stand them in an ovenproof dish.

In a bowl, mix together the blackberries, almonds, allspice, lemon rind, and sugar. Using a teaspoon, spoon the mixture into the center of each apple.

Pour the port into the dish around the apples, add the cinnamon stick, and bake the apples in the preheated oven for 35–40 minutes, or until tender and soft.

Drain the cooking juices into a pan and keep the apples warm.

Discard the cinnamon and add the cornstarch mixture to the cooking juices. Cook over medium heat, stirring constantly, until thickened.

Heat the custard until piping hot. To serve, pour the sauce over the apples and hand round the custard separately.

apples in red wine

serves 4

10 minutes

about 25 minutes

4 eating apples
2 tbsp lemon juice
3 tbsp lowfat spread
scant ⅓ cup raw brown sugar
1 small orange

1 cinnamon stick, broken
⅔ cup red wine
1½ cups raspberries, hulled and
thawed if frozen
fresh mint sprigs, to decorate

This simple combination of apples and raspberries cooked in red wine is a colorful and tempting dessert.

variation

For other fruity combinations, cook the apples with blackberries, black currants, or red currants. You may need to add more sugar if you use currants as they are not so sweet as raspberries.

Peel and core the apples, then cut them into thick wedges. Put the apples into a bowl and toss thoroughly in the lemon juice to prevent the fruit from turning brown.

In a skillet, gently melt the lowfat spread over low heat, add the sugar, and stir to form a paste.

Stir the apple wedges into the pan and cook, stirring, for 2 minutes until well coated in the sugar paste.

Using a vegetable peeler, pare off a few strips of orange rind. Add the orange rind to the pan with the cinnamon pieces. Squeeze the juice from the orange and pour into the pan with the red wine. Bring to a boil, then simmer for 10 minutes, stirring constantly.

Add the raspberries and cook for 5 minutes, or until the apples are tender.

Discard the orange rind and cinnamon pieces. Transfer the apple and raspberry mixture to a serving plate with the wine sauce. Decorate with a mint sprig and serve hot.

baked **bananas**

serves 4

5–10 minutes

about 10 minutes

4 bananas
2 passion fruit
4 tbsp orange juice
4 tbsp orange-flavored liqueur

orange-flavored cream

2/3 cup heavy cream
3 tbsp confectioner's sugar
2 tbsp orange-flavored liqueur

The orange-flavored cream can be prepared in advance, but do not make up the banana pockets until just before you need to cook them.

variation

Leave the bananas in their skins for a really quick dessert. Split the banana skins and pop in 1–2 squares of chocolate. Wrap the bananas in foil and bake for 10 minutes or until the chocolate has just melted.

To make the orange-flavored cream, pour the cream into a mixing bowl and sprinkle over the sugar. Whisk the mixture until it is standing in soft peaks. Carefully fold in the orange-flavored liqueur and chill in the refrigerator until required.

Preheat the oven to 350°F/180°C. Peel the bananas and put each one on a sheet of foil.

Cut the passion fruit in half and squeeze the juice of each half over each banana. Spoon over the orange juice and liqueur.

Fold the foil over the top of the bananas so that they are completely enclosed.

Put the pockets on a cookie sheet and bake the bananas in the preheated oven for 10 minutes, or until they are just tender (test by inserting a toothpick).

Transfer the foil pockets to warm, individual serving plates. Open out the foil pockets at the table and then serve immediately with the chilled orange-flavored cream.

exotic fruit pockets

serves 4

10–15 minutes, plus 30 minutes marinating

15–20 minutes

1 papaya
1 mango
1 carambola
1 tbsp grenadine

3 tbsp orange juice
light cream or plain yogurt, to serve

Delicious pieces of exotic fruit are warmed through in a wonderfully scented sauce to make a fabulous and simple dessert.

cook's tip

Grenadine is a sweet syrup made from pomegranates. If you prefer you could use pomegranate juice instead. To extract the juice, cut the pomegranate in half and squeeze gently with a lemon squeezer—do not press too hard or the juice may become bitter.

Cut the papaya in half, scoop out the seeds, and discard them. Peel the papaya and cut the flesh into thick slices.

Prepare the mango by cutting it in half lengthwise and cutting carefully away from the flat central pit.

Score each mango half in a criss-cross pattern. Push each mango half inside out to separate the cubes and cut them away from the peel.

Using a sharp knife, thickly slice the carambola.

Put all of the fruit in a bowl and mix them together.

Mix the grenadine and orange juice together and pour over the fruits. Let marinate for at least 30 minutes.

Divide the fruits among 4 double-thickness squares of foil and gather up the edges to form a pocket that encloses the fruit.

Put the foil pocket on a rack set over warm coals and grill the fruits for 15–20 minutes.

Serve the fruits in the pocket with light cream or plain yogurt.

Index